TESS OF THE D'URBERVILLES

NOTES

including
- *Biographical and Critical Introduction*
- *List of Characters*
- *Synopsis of the Story*
- *Chapter Summaries and Commentaries*
- *Analysis and Discussion*
- *Character Analyses*
- *Glossary*
- *Suggested Examination Questions*
- *Selected Bibliography*

by
Lorraine M. Force

INCORPORATED

LINCOLN, NEBRASKA   68501

Editor

Gary Carey, M.A.
University of Colorado

Consulting Editor

James L. Roberts, Ph.D.
Department of English
University of Nebraska

4/00 Moonbeam Pub./5.00

ISBN 0-8220-1273-1
© Copyright 1966
by
Cliffs Notes, Inc.
All Rights Reserved
Printed in U.S.A.

1999 Printing

Cliffs Notes, Inc.   Lincoln, Nebraska

CONTENTS

CONTENTS

TESS OF THE D'URBERVILLES

BIOGRAPHY OF THOMAS HARDY

Thomas Hardy was born on June 2, 1840, in Higher Bockhampton, Stinsford, Dorset, England, the eldest of four children. His father made his living in a building and masoning business which his grandfather had started.

Hardy was a healthy, but fragile child who could read almost before he could walk. He showed an unusual sensitivity to music, which was an important part of his family's life. For forty years his grandfather, father, and uncle provided the music for the Stinsford Church. When he was older, Hardy often played the dance fiddle with his father and uncle for weddings and dances.

He was sent to the village school when he was eight, and the following few years were spent in the Dorchester Day School, a nonconformist school for its day. He began the study of Latin at the age of twelve and continued it along with his other studies for several years.

When he was sixteen he became a student of John Hicks', a Dorchester architect and church restorer. With remarkable self-discipline he developed his classical education by studying Greek between the hours of four and eight in the morning. During this period he became acquainted with two men of letters who were to influence him: the Reverend William Barnes, a Dorset poet and philologist, who "kept school" next to Hicks' office; and Horace Moule, of Queen's College, Cambridge, an author and reviewer. Hardy began to write poetry when he was seventeen and Moule's serious but kindly criticism meant much to Hardy.

In 1862 Hardy went to London to work for an architect, Arthur Blomfield. He wrote some poetry, which he could not get published, and read a good deal. After a few years ill health forced him to leave London and in 1867 he went back to work for Hicks. He began writing prose about this time, and although his first novel, *The Poor Man and the Lady* was rejected by the publishers, it brought encouragement. George Meredith, a critic for Macmillans, advised him to soften his social satire or write another novel with a more complicated plot. In 1870 Hardy's last job as an architect, the restoration at St. Juliot in Cornwall, brought him a wife, for it was there he met Emma Lavinia Gifford, whom he married in 1874.

His first published novel was *Desperate Remedies* in 1871, for which he had to advance 75 pounds, most of which was returned after publication. Tinsley Brothers also published his second novel, *Under the Greenwood Tree*, in 1872 and the following year ran *A Pair of Blue Eyes* as a serial in *Tinsley's Magazine*. The reviews tended to be favorable and more requests for serials came. Although he continued to write some poetry, for the next fifteen years he concentrated on writing novels, among them *Far From the Madding Crowd* (1874), *The Return of the Native* (1878), and *The Mayor of Casterbridge* (1886).

Hardy and his wife spent three or four months of each year in London, but the majority of his time was spent in the country near the place of his birth. In 1883 he oversaw the building of his house at Max Gate near Dorchester, where he was to live until his death.

Tess was begun in 1889 and was refused by two publishers. Hardy consequently altered his story to make it suitable for family readers and in July, 1891, it began running as a serial in the *Graphic* in England and in *Harper's Bazaar*, the leading family paper of its time in America. Although it met with general acceptance and lifted Hardy to a position of world fame, it was to be one of his last novels. The stormy reaction to *Jude the Obscure*, published in 1894, caused him to abandon novel writing and his last novel, *The Well Beloved*, appeared in 1897. From then on he concentrated on short stories and poetry and a major work, published in 1903-8, *The Dynasts: A Drama of the Napoleonic Wars*. His final volume of verse, *Winter Words*, appeared in 1928.

In 1912 his wife died, and in 1914 he married Florence Emily Dugdale. He had no children. Hardy died January 11, 1928. He was buried in Westminster Abbey. His heart, in a separate casket, was buried at Stinsford near the graves of his ancestors and his first wife.

A great many honors came to Hardy during his lifetime, including degrees and honorary fellowships bestowed by Oxford and Cambridge. In 1910 the King awarded him the Order of Merit. A volume of tributes by living poets was presented to him in 1918.

Tess was dramatized in 1897 in America and in 1924 it was produced successfully by "The Hardy Players" in Dorset and Weymouth and then ran for several months in London.

HARDY'S PHILOSOPHY AND IDEAS

Hardy is primarily a storyteller and should be viewed more as a chronicler of moods and deeds than as a philosopher. Yet a novel such as *Tess*, which raises many questions about society, religion, morals, and the contrast between a good life and its rewards, is bound to make the reader curious about the author who brings them up.

Hardy lived in an age of transition which added to his natural disposition toward a melancholy view of life. The industrial revolution was in the process of destroying the agricultural life and the subsequent shifting of population caused a disintegration of rural customs and traditions which had meant security, stability, and dignity for the people. It was a period when fundamental beliefs—religious, social, scientific, and political—were shaken to their very core and brought in their stead the "ache of modernism."

The new philosophies failed to satisfy the emotional needs of people as religion had done. Hardy as a young man read Darwin's *Origin of the Species* and *Essays and Reviews* (the manifesto of a few churchmen who held radical theological opinions), both of which were to influence his views toward religion. He found it difficult, if not impossible, to reconcile the idea of a beneficent, omnipotent, and omniscient diety with the fact of omnipresent evil and persistent tendency of circumstances toward unhappiness. And so we find in *Tess* the great conflict is between her inherent will to enjoy and the circumstantial forces which are indifferent to her wishes and efforts.

Hardy considered himself a "meliorist" until 1914, when the absurdity and horror of war shattered his belief that the universal scheme was gradually changing for the better.

FATALISM

When one thinks of Hardy the novelist, that aspect of his work which comes to mind most readily is his frequent use of chance and circumstance in the development of his plots. But the reader must view his stories, and *Tess* specifically, in the light of the author's fatalistic outlook on life.

Hardy fluctuates between fatalism and determinism: fatalism being that view of life which says that all action is controlled by the nature of things or by Fate which is a great, impersonal, primitive force existing through all eternity, absolutely independent of human wills and superior to any god created by man; determinism, while acknowledging that man's struggle against the will behind things is of no avail, does decree that the laws of cause and effect are in operation. The human will is not free and the human being has no control over his own destiny, try as he may. The source of happiness is not within us but rather rests with external manifestations of the universal force. Hardy sees life in terms of action, in the doomed struggle against the circumstantial forces against happiness. Incident plays an important role in causing joy or pain and often an act of indiscretion in early youth can wreck the chances for happiness. Within a man's goodness may lie his own undoing; almost every step in Tess's undoing has its origin in a lofty motive and worthy trait of character.

Fate appears as an artistic motif in a great variety of forms: chance and coincidence, nature, time, woman, and convention. None is Fate itself, but rather all of these are manifestations of the Immanent Will.

The use of chance and coincidence as a means of furthering the plot was a technique used by many Victorian authors but with Hardy it becomes something more than a mere device. Fateful incidents, overheard conversations, and undelivered letters symbolize the forces working against mere man in his efforts to control his own destiny. Many examples of the fateful incident may be found in *Tess:* Tess's misfortune to be born first into a shiftless family; Durbeyfield's learning of his lineage; the death of the horse; the events which frustrate Tess's attempt to confess to Angel, ending in her letter slipping beneath the carpet; the death of her father; and the return of Angel just too late. One has the impression this is a book of "what might have been": if Angel had danced with Tess the first time he saw her, what a different story this would have been; if Angel had not caught sight of the portrait of the d'Urberville lady outside Tess's chamber, he probably would have weakened and entered the room with altogether different results; or if Tess had not overheard the conversation of Angel's brothers and had instead followed through on her plans to visit his parents, she probably would not have met Alec again and her entire life would have been changed.

Fate appears in the form of nature, endowing it with varying moods which affect the lives of the characters. Those who are most in harmony with their environment are usually the most contented and those who can appreciate the joys of nature can find solace in it from their cares. But nature can take on sinister aspects, becoming more of an actor than just a setting for the action. "The night came in, and took up its place there, unconcerned and indifferent; the night which had already swallowed up his happiness, and was now digesting it listlessly; and was ready to swallow up the happiness of a thousand other people with as little disturbance or change of mien" (Chapter 35).

Time, also, is used as a motif of Fate. There is tremendous importance placed on the moment, for time is a great series of moments. The joys of life are transitory and the moments of joy may be turned to bitterness by time. Love, that universal symbol of happiness, may be changed by time. For example, when Angel and Tess knew that "though the fascination which each had exercised over the other...would probably in the first days of their separation be even more potent than ever, time must attenuate that effect" (Chapter 36).

When Tess meets Alec: "Had she perceived this meeting's import she might have asked why she was *doomed* to be seen and coveted *that day* by the wrong man, and not by some other man, the right and desired one in all respects" (Chapter 5).

Woman is Fate's most potent instrument for opposing Man's happiness. Closer to primitive feelings than Man, Woman is helpless in the hands of Fate and carries out Fate's work. In her search for love, the motivating passion of her life, Woman becomes an agent in her own destiny. Tess and the dairymaids are vessels of emotion: for example, "The air of the sleeping-chamber seemed to palpitate with the hopeless passion of the girls. They writhed feverishly under the oppressiveness of an emotion thrust on them by cruel Nature's law—an emotion which they had neither expected nor desired.... The differences which distinguished them as individuals were abstracted by this passion, and each was but portion of one organism called sex" (Chapter 23).

Perhaps the most ironic manifestation of Fate as used by Hardy is that of convention. Convention and Law can work as effectively against Man as the other aspects of Fate, yet these are devised by Man himself. Man is powerless to change the other workings of Fate; but those which are contrived by Man and which work against him can be changed by Man. Thus we see in *Tess* a desperate cry against those evils which can and must be corrected. The social laws must be brought into accord with natural law. There are many examples of Hardy's rebukes against society and conventions. "She might have seen that what had bowed her head so profoundly—the thought of the world's concern at her situation—was founded on an illusion. She was not an existence, an experience, a passion, a structure of sensations to anybody but herself. To all humankind, Tess was only a passing thought.... Moreover, alone in a desert island would she have been wretched at what had happened to her? Not greatly. If she could have been created, to discover herself as a spouseless mother, with no experience of life except as a parent of a nameless child, would the position have caused her to despair? No, she would have taken it calmly, and found pleasures therein. Most of the misery had been generated by her conventional aspect, and not by her innate sensations" (Chapter 14). "She was ashamed of herself for her gloom of the night, based on nothing more tangible than a sense of condemnation under an arbitrary law of society which had no foundation in Nature" (Chapter 41).

Angel Clare personifies the role convention can play in shaping one's destiny (for a discussion of this character, see "Character Analyses").

To the Wessex rustic, Fate is also revealed by means of many omens and signs. Joan lives by her fortune-telling book, although she is afraid to have it in the house while she sleeps. Almost everything has significance: the cows will not let down their milk, the butter will not come in the churn, the cock crows in the afternoon. The vision of the d'Urberville Coach is a bad omen, as is the stone of the "Cross-in-Hand." Fate is a part of life, and hence much can be explained away. Angel chooses Tess, but it is really Fate which has made the choice; therefore, the dairymaids do not blame Tess for any part of it. Marian says it must be something outside both Angel and Tess which has caused their separation, for she knows neither of them has any faults. It "was to be" that Alec should seduce Tess, that is, she is not to blame.

STRUCTURE AND PLOT

Tess of the d'Urbervilles is a novel about Tess from the time she is sixteen or seventeen to the age of about twenty-one. Using what has been termed an epic form, Hardy has described her life during this period. There is a continuity of events from the time we meet her until she dies. We are told of her actions, her justifications for them, her trials and tribulations, and her efforts to overcome the circumstantial will against enjoyment. Other characters must, of course, come into the story, but only what is important to Tess is told us. There are no subplots which interweave with the main story; only Tess's story is important. She as a human being is explored thoroughly, both emotionally and intellectually. Those events which have significance in her life are examined carefully.

The novel is divided into seven phases, at the end of each a fateful incident has changed Tess's life. She begins each phase of her life with an altered view of herself and her destiny.

The plot of *Tess* is one of the simplest that Hardy ever devised: the woman sins, the woman pays. This plot was used by innumerable Victorian authors whose names will never be remembered. In the hands of Hardy, however, this hackneyed pattern is formed into a work of art. Hardy denies and challenges two traditional themes: (1) the stain of unchastity can never be erased and (2) the pious possibility of purifying atonement. By taking the sentimental pattern and coating it with irony, Hardy is able to evoke reactions to situations opposite to the usual ones. His woman is presented as innately pure, before and after her "sin." She is absolved of responsibility for her fall, being but a child untutored in the dangers of men. Should she suffer for this eternally? The reader, impressed by her courage and nobility of character, shouts, "No!"

Hardy's plot is primarily one of action, for he sees life as a series of actions. It must not, however, be commonplace, or it will not sustain the interest of the reader. He, therefore, includes the fantastic, the surprising, that which will strike the imagination of the reader. In a few instances in this book he stretches the limits of credulity of the reader, for example, the sleepwalking scene. Chance and coincidence, which are discussed more fully above, play such a large part in his plots that at times they seem contrived.

LIST OF CHARACTERS

Tess Durbeyfield

The heroine of the novel; her life exemplifies the clash between "the inherent will to enjoy and the circumstantial forces against enjoyment." Intelligent, attractive, and naturally dignified, she is sixteen years old at the beginning of the story.

John Durbeyfield

Tess's father, whose natural aversion to work is intensified by the discovery that he is descended from an ancient noble family.

Joan Durbeyfield

Tess's mother; simple-minded and phelgmatic, she is little affected by the blows of misfortune.

Eliza Louisa ('Liza Lu) Durbeyfield

The Durbeyfield's second child. She is twelve years of age at the beginning of the story.

Abraham Durbeyfield

Tess's small brother; he is nine years old when the story begins. He is the third of the Durbeyfield's seven children.

Sorrow

Tess's child, who died in infancy.

Alec d'Urberville

The son of Simon Stoke. His talents range from seduction to evangelical preaching.

Mrs. d'Urberville

The blind widow of Simon Stoke. She is mistress of "The Slopes," a mansion built by her husband after he retired from business in the North of England and assumed the name of the ancient d'Urbervilles.

Angel Clare

Youngest son of the Reverend Mr. Clare of Emminster. Being too liberal in his thinking to prepare for the ministry, he turned to agriculture for a career.

The Reverend Mr. Clare of Emminster

Angel's father, a self-sacrificing clergyman of charitable sentiments but rigid opinions.

Mrs. Clare

Angel's mother, a kindhearted woman somewhat inclined to be swayed by the values of a class-conscious society.

The Reverend Felix Clare

Brother of Angel who is a curate.

The Reverend Cuthbert Clare

Brother of Angel who is a classical scholar, and fellow and dean of his college at Cambridge.

Mercy Chant

Daughter of friend and neighbor of the Reverend Mr. Clare, who would like to have Angel marry her. She is finally betrothed to Angel's brother Cuthbert.

Richard Crick
The master-dairyman of Talbothays.

Marian
Milkmaid at Talbothays. Love for Angel Clare leads to her drinking after he marries Tess. She later gets Tess a job at Flintcomb-Ash.

Izz Huett
Milkmaid at Talbothays. Angel Clare impulsively invites her to go to Brazil with him after he abandons Tess.

Retty Priddle
Milkmaid at Talbothays. Her love for Angel Clare results in her conspicuous decline after he marries Tess.

SYNOPSIS OF THE STORY

Upon learning that they are descended from an illustrious family, the struggling Durbeyfields send their eldest daughter, Tess, to seek help from the rich Mrs. d'Urberville, whom they believe to be a relative. The d'Urbervilles are, in fact, no relation, but Tess does not realize this when she meets Alec d'Urberville, the son, who is impressed with her beauty and offers to find some way to help her. He sends a letter to the family offering Tess a job tending fowls on his mother's estate. Tess is reluctant to go, but she feels responsible for the plight of her family and finally agrees to go to Trantridge. After several months Alec takes advantage of her in the woods one night, and she remains with him for a few weeks longer.

Tess realizes that she doesn't love Alec and hates herself for her weakness. She returns to her home where after some months she bears Alec's child, who dies shortly after birth. For the next year or so Tess remains at home, but finally decides that perhaps she can find happiness if she leaves Marlott. She leaves home once again, this time to work as a dairymaid at the Talbothays Dairy.

At the dairy Tess hopes to lay the foundation for a new life and is alarmed to recognize an apprentice dairyman as a man who once saw her in Marlott. Angel Clare has a vague recollection of seeing her before, but is more impressed with her freshness and purity. They become interested in each other and their relationship develops as the summer wears on. Angel declares his love for Tess and asks her to marry him. Tess is deeply in love with Angel and is happier than she has ever been, but feels it is not right for her to accept his proposal. She tries to tell him about her past life but cannot risk her chance for happiness. She accepts his proposal and the date for the wedding is set.

Tess tries again to confess to Angel by writing him a letter which she slips under his door, but the letter goes under the carpet and he never sees it. He tells her they will both confess after they are married. Accordingly, following their wedding, Angel tells Tess about a brief involvement he once had with an older woman. Tess forgives him and tells him about her affair with Alec d'Urberville. But Angel cannot forgive Tess and for a few days they live as strangers in the same house while Angel thinks of a plan. At last Tess offers to go home and Angel tells her not to come to him until he comes for her, but that she may write if she needs anything.

Keeping the reason for the estrangement secret from her parents, Tess gives them half of the money Angel has given her and leaves their house. Meanwhile Angel decides to go to Brazil to try his luck at farming there. Tess is able to find work as she needs it, until after the harvest when her money is gone. She joins a friend from the dairy who has a job on a poor farm for the winter.

Tess has not heard from Angel for a long time and decides to visit his family one Sunday. She reaches the vicarage after a long walk only to overhear Angel's brothers discussing his unfortunate marriage. On her return to the farm she stops to hear a wandering preacher who turns out to be Alec. He tells her his conversion has been brought about by Mr. Clare, Angel's father. He makes her swear she will never tempt him by her charms or ways.

A few days later Alec approaches Tess in the field while she is working and asks her to marry him. She tells him she is married and begs him to leave. After seeing Tess a few times, Alec renounces his preaching and suggests that Tess will succumb to him once again. Tess writes to Angel imploring him to come home and help her.

Tess's sister appears at the farm one night to tell her that their mother is dying and Tess leaves immediately for her home. But within a short time, the mother is recovering and the father dies. Upon his death the family is turned out of the house and the mother decides they will go to Kingsbere, the site of the former d'Urberville greatness. Alec has offered help of various kinds to the family, but Tess won't accept.

As a result of the hardships which he has suffered in Brazil and a more enlightened attitude, Angel has changed his opinion of Tess and he begins his journey home. When he reaches England he is tired and ill but sets out within a few days to find Tess. He finally finds her mother, who reluctantly tells him that Tess is at Sandbourne. Angel finds Tess in a fashionable boardinghouse and tells her he has forgiven her. She tells him he has come too late and asks him to go away. He leaves and she returns to the bedroom, where she kills Alec and then rushes to catch up with Angel. They are reconciled at last but follow backroads to escape discovery. They spend a few blissful days in a deserted mansion before they take off again. They come at last to Stonehenge, where Tess makes Angel promise he will take care of her sister and perhaps marry her if anything should happen to Tess. They are discovered and Tess is taken away to prison where she is put to death.

PHASE THE FIRST: THE MAIDEN

CHAPTERS 1, 2, 3

Summary

As the peddler, John Durbeyfield, returns to his village of Marlott, he is greeted by an elderly parson who addresses him, "Sir John." In answer to the puzzled man's question, Parson Tringham explains that he is an antiquary and that recently he has discovered that the Durbeyfields are the descendants of the ancient and knightly family of d'Urbervilles. He informs Durbeyfield that they are extinct as a county family, that neither land nor fortunes remain in the family, and that only their crypts remain in the church at Kingsbere. He tells Durbeyfield the information is of interest only to historians.

But to John Durbeyfield this disclosure raises his self-esteem and within a short time he has sent a boy to fetch a horse and carriage to carry him home. Waving his hand above his head, he chants slowly, "I've-got-a-gr't-family-vault-at-Kingsbere — and knighted-forefathers-in-lead-coffins-there!"

He is seen by his daughter, Tess, who is participating in the annual May Day procession and dance with other women from the village. She is embarrassed by the spectacle her father makes but will not tolerate her companions' amused remarks. She accompanies them to the green, where the dancing begins among the women. Joining the onlookers are three brothers, of a superior class, who are hiking through the valley. The older two are anxious to be on their way, but the youngest stays for a while to dance.

He does not dance with Tess but notices her as he is leaving and sees that she watches him as he hurries to catch up with his brothers. He wishes he had danced with her, but since it could not be helped, he thinks no more about it.

Tess lingers until the stranger can no longer be seen and then joins in the dancing. She remains with her companions until dusk, when she remembers the strange appearance of her father earlier in the afternoon and hurries home. Her mother tells her about their illustrious ancestors and that her father has learned that day that he has a serious heart condition. He has gone to Rolliver's Inn to get up his strength for the trip he must take with a load of beehives shortly after midnight.

Tess is alarmed at this news and rebukes her mother for letting him go to the inn. She offers to fetch him, but her mother has her coat and hat ready and is looking forward to a few minutes away from family cares. Tess is left to look after the younger children. When it grows late, she sends her young brother to bring home her parents. When he does not return, she goes to get them herself.

Commentary

The disclosure that the Durbeyfields are related to the noteworthy d'Urberville family is made at the beginning of Chapter 1 and immediately the reader is made aware that henceforth things will be different for Tess's family. John has heard that his family has seen better days, but has not thought about it until the authority tells him it is true. No longer will he be content to be John Durbeyfield, the peddler. He feels he has been denied his rightful heritage and tries to live as he believes his knightly ancestors did. The mother, steeped in superstition and folklore, consults her fortune-telling book and gives her imagination wide range. She expects many rich relatives to come calling, and as we shall soon see, she anticipates regaining their place among the aristocracy through Tess.

The setting is very important in Hardy novels. Taking place in Wessex, Hardy's imaginary county, the story begins in the valley in which the heroine was born and raised. Hardy shows us the Valley of Blackmoor as an isolated area which differs sharply from the country beyond the encircling hills. "Here, in the valley, the world seems to be constructed upon a smaller and more delicate scale." By describing Tess's world as a small, sheltered, and isolated place, Hardy adds to his portrait of Tess as a simple country maiden who is protected from and innocent of the dangers of the world beyond.

In Chapter 3 we see excellent examples of the interaction of the setting with the action and the mood of the scene, a favorite technique of Hardy. Tess returns "from the holiday gaieties of the field—the white gowns, the nosegays, the willow wands, the whirling movements on the green, the flash of gentle sentiment towards the stranger—to the yellow melancholy of this one-candled spectacle, what a step!" A little later she rebukes her mother for letting her father go to a public house to get up his strength. "Her rebuke and her mood seemed to fill the whole room, and to impart a cowed look to the furniture, and candle, and children playing about, and to her mother's face."

Our first picture of Tess is one of a pretty and innocent country girl who is shy and modest. Her pride and family loyalty are important qualities which help lead to her tragedy. She is contrasted with her shiftless parents and shown to be the responsible member of the family.

Tess is attracted to Angel at first sight; his manners are so much nicer than those of the village boys. Angel is viewed as an intruder into the life of the village. He and his brothers are described as being "of a superior class," as temporary visitors to the village of Marlott. Less concerned than his brothers with social conventions, Angel is amused by the brief diversion from their walking tour.

CHAPTER 4

Summary

At Rolliver's Inn Mrs. Durbeyfield tells her husband of her plan to send Tess to "claim Kin" with the rich Mrs. d'Urberville who lives near Trantridge. According to her fortune-telling book, this trip will lead to a grand and noble marriage for Tess. Abraham overhears this conversation while waiting for his parents, who hurriedly leave the inn when Tess appears. John's poor health combined with a few drinks make him unable to take the load of bees to market. Tess, rather than have anyone else know why her father is not going, decides to take the wagon herself with Abraham to keep her company. During the ride Abraham tells Tess of the family's plan for her to marry a rich gentleman. Tess allows him to go to sleep and soon falls asleep herself. Before daylight they are awakened by an accident in which the mail-cart has killed their old horse. A farmer is sent to take them on to market and later to take the horse to Marlott. Tess is overcome with remorse and blames herself for the loss of the family's livelihood far more than her unambitious parents blame her. Her father works harder digging a grave for Prince than he has worked for months growing food for his family.

Commentary

Tess's relationship to her family is clearly shown in this chapter. She is the responsible member, the one who carries the burden of the family. Her guilt at the loss of Prince is intensified because she is the only one who realizes just what it means to the future of the family.

Hardy describes the countryside with such faithfulness that many of his readers were able to retrace the journeys of his characters. Along with his fine ear for the speech of the country people, this ability to portray the scenery in such detail added to Hardy's popularity. The realism of the setting is intensified by the poet's ability to describe beyond what can be seen. For example, the bedroom in the inn takes on the mellow glow of the drinking inhabitants: "The chamber and its furniture grew more and more dignified and luxurious; the shawl hanging at the window took upon itself the richness of tapestry; the brass handles of the chest of drawers were as golden knockers; and the carved bedposts seemed to have some kinship with the magnificent pillars of Solomon's temple."

Tess is impatient with her family's plan to marry her to a gentleman; she is more concerned with the cares of today than with dreams of ancient glory or visions of future nobility. We see that Tess at seventeen is already resigned to a hard life.

CHAPTERS 5, 6, 7

Summary

Tess's feeling of guilt regarding the death of the horse makes her more amenable to her mother's plan for her to visit Mrs. d'Urberville. She doesn't relish the role of poor relation but she does agree to visit the relative. Expecting an ancient mansion, Tess is surprised and somewhat alarmed at the sight of a new and well-equipped residence built strictly for pleasure. What she does not know is that this is the house built by Simon Stoke upon his retirement as a merchant; in order to disassociate himself from his past when he settles here, he takes on the name of d'Urberville.

Tess is even more surprised at the appearance of young Alec d'Urberville, who tells her his mother is an invalid and learns the purpose of her visit. Impressed by the beauty and ample figure of the girl and amused by the incident, he tells her he will try to do something for her.

By the time Tess reaches home a letter has already arrived offering her a job tending fowls for the d'Urbervilles. Tess is suspicious of the offer but after a week of trying to find employment in Marlott, she at last consents to go to Trantridge. She thinks only of being able to earn enough money to buy a new horse.

On the morning of Tess's departure, Joan insists that Tess dress in her best clothes. The mother has some misgivings about the venture and walks a ways with Tess accompanied by a couple of the children. After a hasty good-bye, Tess approaches the cart sent for her luggage. Before she reaches it, Alec appears in a fancy gig and urges her to get up beside him. Tess can still see her family; her misgivings are thrust aside at the sight of them, and she steps into the gig. As soon as she is out of sight the children begin to cry and Joan wishes she had found out more about the young man.

Commentary

The author's musings about Fate in Chapter 5 give the reader a clue regarding the outcome of the meeting between Tess and Alec. Why wasn't Tess seen that day by Angel? Fate — the great, impersonal, primitive force which shapes man's destiny — is manifested in this instance as Time. "Had she perceived this meeting's import she might have asked why she was *doomed* to be seen and coveted *that day* by the wrong man, and not by some other man, the right and desired one in all respects.... In the ill-judged execution of the well-judged plan of things the call seldom produces the comer, the man to love rarely coincides with the *hour* for loving.... in the present case.... it was not the two halves of a perfect whole that confronted each other at the *perfect* moment; a missing counterpart wandered independently about the earth waiting in crass obtuseness till the *late time* came. Out of which maladroit *delay* sprang anxieties, disappointments, shocks, catastrophes, and passing-strange *destinies*."

Step by step, Tess is moving down the path to her own undoing. The author carefully shows us the lofty motives and worthy traits of character which move her along. Because she wants to help her family out of its predicament, she agrees to go along with a plan which she instinctively dislikes. Her misgivings about Alec are well founded, but her sense of responsibility for her family's welfare causes her to disregard them.

Our first picture of Alec is calculated to deepen the suspicion regarding his motives. The reader can almost picture the villain in a melodrama. We see him just as Tess sees him; the author provides no additional information regarding his past or his character to enable the reader to form a different opinion concerning him.

CHAPTERS 8, 9

Summary

Alec frightens Tess with his reckless driving, and she implores him to stop. He promises that he will if she will let him kiss her. Distressed, she agrees. She instinctively wipes the kiss off her cheek, and Alec becomes very angry. When her hat blows off, Tess gets down to get it and refuses to return to the cart. Alec swears at her and Tess's temper flares. The rest of the journey is made on foot by Tess with Alec riding in the cart beside her.

The next morning Tess is summoned by Mrs. d'Urberville, who is blind. In addition to tending the fowls, Mrs. d'Urberville asks Tess to whistle to her bullfinches every morning. Alec helps her regain her former ability to whistle and Tess settles into the pleasant routine of her new position.

Commentary

Tess's lofty resolve to help her family causes her to accept more abuse from Alec than she might in different circumstances. She wants to go home but feels that her reasons would be considered childish. Tess's temper is aroused by Alec as by no other person and will be shown several times in the novel. Alec likes her better when she shows spirit; he vacillates between wanting to master her and having her like him. Alec is somewhat distressed at the sight of her walking, for which he is to blame.

Tess does not realize that Mrs. d'Urberville knows nothing of the supposed kinship between them. Tess thinks the old woman's indifferent manner toward her is quite fitting for the mistress of such a great house. Alec playfully calls her cousin only when they are alone. Tess becomes accustomed to Alec's presence, but the author tells us only in summary of their relationship during the next few weeks.

CHAPTERS 10, 11

Summary

One Saturday in September Tess goes to the weekly market at Chaseborough and finds that it is also the day of a fair. As usual, she waits for companions for the walk home at night but finds that they have all gone to a private dance. They assure her they will not be long, and she prefers their company and protection to that of Alec, who offers to give her a ride home. When they finally do start home, some of them are intoxicated. A row begins between Tess and the former recipients of d'Urberville's attentions.

Tess is ready to flee from the group when Alec arrives and offers her a ride on his horse. By the time the group realizes what has happened, the two are speeding away.

By this time Tess is inexpressibly weary and does not notice that Alec lets the horse turn at random in order to prolong his ride with her. He asks that he be allowed to treat her as a lover but she still distrusts him. When she finally realizes that they are off the road to Trantridge, Alec himself is not sure where they are. He leaves her by the horse while he searches for some landmark. First he tells her that he has provided her father with a new horse and sent some toys for the children. The fog thickens and by the time Alec returns, Tess is asleep.

Commentary

Tess is divided into seven phases. At the end of each phase, Tess has reached a juncture in her life; circumstances have changed her life so that she will be different henceforth.

The implication at the end of this chapter is that "the woman has fallen." But note how the author portrays Tess as blameless—an innocent taken advantage of by a rather sinister man.

The scene is carefully set for the seduction of Tess. She has worked hard and long hours all week, and on this evening has walked the three miles to town and waited three hours for her companions without eating or drinking. Despite the tardiness of her friends, she prefers their company to that of Alec and refuses his first offer of a ride home. She walks at least a mile of the way home before the quarrel ensues, brought about by the jealousy of two women who formerly had received Alec's attentions. At almost any other time, Tess would have refused Alec's offer of help, but his appearance at a moment when "fear and indignation at these adversaries could be transformed by a spring of the foot into a triumph over them" causes her to accept impulsively.

Poor innocent Tess! For the first time she realizes that Alec's passion for her is a factor in his generous gifts to her family. Alec's willingness to help Tess's family is his hold over Tess. As will be seen several times in this story, his provision of material aid to the impoverished family makes Tess beholden to him. She makes a valiant effort to be independent of him, but in the end the struggle is too much for her.

PHASE THE SECOND: MAIDEN NO MORE

CHAPTERS 12, 13

Summary

A few weeks later Tess can be seen, laden with her belongings, on the road to Marlott. She is overtaken by Alec, who has discovered her absence and has driven to take her the rest of the way if she won't return to him. She tells him that she won't return, she doesn't love him, and she will not accept his offers of material help. Telling her that she should let him know if any difficulty arises and advising her to show her beauty to the world before it fades, Alec takes his leave.

When Tess tells her mother what has happened, her mother is disgusted with her for not marrying Alec. She tells Tess she should have been more careful, but Tess points out to her that she did not know the danger and that her mother did not help her. Her mother decides to make the best of it.

Several friends come to call that afternoon, eager to see Tess, whom they believe to have made a great conquest. She grows almost gay in their company but the next morning she is terribly depressed and sees her future as a "long and stony highway which she must tread, without aid, and with little sympathy." In a few weeks she goes to church one Sunday but is so embarrassed by people's whispering about her that she retreats to her home only to emerge after dark for walks in the woods.

Commentary

Tess is overcome with remorse and reproaches herself for her weakness. We learn in Chapter 12 that she stays with Alec for a few weeks; her "eyes were dazed by [him] for a little" and she "didn't understand [his] meaning till it was too late." The author continues to emphasize her innocence in the affair: she "succumbed to adroit advantages he took of her helplessness; then, temporarily blinded by his ardent manners, had been stirred to confused surrender awhile: had suddenly despised and disliked him, and had run away."

Her honesty and pride prevent her from lying to Alec about loving him although she realizes that she would gain from this falsehood. He has not mentioned marriage but she probably would not have accepted his offer even for the sake of her reputation. She blames her mother in part for not warning her about the possible dangers facing her, but most of the blame she reserves for herself.

The author contrasts Tess before and after the affair. Leaving Trantridge she is no longer the simple girl who arrived four months previously and her "views of life have been totally changed." The author also intensifies his portrait of her as innocent by emphasizing that Tess has broken a social law, not a natural one, and that most of her distress is caused by her fear of "moral hobgoblins."

The sign painter appears several times in the novel. He represents the moral life as spelled out in the Bible. His signs point the accusatory finger of social convention at a character, and in this instance his appearance intensifies Tess's feelings of guilt and remorse. In this chapter we learn that it was Mr. Clare, Angel's father, who started him on this work.

When Tess's temper flares against Alec, the author tells us that Alec will be seen again, that he will once again be the recipient of Tess's emotional outburst. It is interesting to note that even Alec is impressed by her noble manner in refusing to stay with him or to accept material help from him. The sham d'Urberville is contrasted with the true descendant of the family.

CHAPTERS 14, 15

Summary

By August of the following year Tess has exhausted every means of self-reproach, and common sense has impelled her to end her long seclusion and to help with the harvest. At noon one day her siblings bring her infant to her in the fields, where with courage and dignity she nurses him. When she returns home in the evening, she finds that the baby has suddenly become ill in the afternoon and is dying. The baby has not been baptized and Tess wishes to send for the parson, but her father doesn't want anyone prying into their affairs and locks the door. During the night Tess cannot bear the thought that her child will have no salvation and performs a baptismal service herself, in the presence of her young brothers and sisters.

The infant dies the following morning and Tess asks the parson if her christening was sufficient for a Christian burial. Impressed with the girl's dignity and sincerity, the parson tells her he cannot bury the child but that Tess's service and burial will be sufficient. That night the baby is buried in a neglected corner of the churchyard and Tess bravely decorates her child's grave.

Tess realizes that she can never be happy in Marlott and wants to try to find happiness in a place where neither she nor her past are known. An opportunity to work in a dairy arises a year from the following spring. She is resolved to be merely a milkmaid, but she is interested that the Talbothays Dairy lies near the former estates of the d'Urbervilles.

Commentary

Excellent examples may be found in Chapter 14 of Hardy's descriptive powers; the harvest scene is vividly portrayed and the baptismal scene is one of the most moving of the entire book.

Hardy challenges the Victorian notion that once fallen a woman may never rise again. He emphasizes the fact that Tess tortures herself for breaking a social convention far more than her acquaintances would bother to. To them she is but a passing thought.

A chapter of Tess's life is thus closed. She looks forward with hope to her future life — hope brought by the resurgence of her "unexpended youth" and the "invincible instinct towards self-delight."

PHASE THE THIRD: THE RALLY

CHAPERS 16, 17

Summary

Two and a half years after her return from Trantridge, Tess leaves her home again, this time to travel to the Talbothays Dairy. Tess is "in good heart and full of zest for life" and her hopes are high as she reaches the Valley of the Great Dairies. As she views it for the first time she is struck by the differences between it and the valley in which she was raised. She reaches the valley floor as the cows are being called in for milking, and follows the herd to the farmyard.

She is welcomed warmly by the master-dairyman, who is glad to have an extra hand during the busy season. Rather than resting, she joins in the milking and feels she has "really...laid a new foundation for her future." One of the men stands out from the rest and with a start she recognizes him as the stranger who joined in the dance in Marlott some years before. Her fears that he might somehow discover her story are allayed when he shows no sign of remembering her. That evening in the quarters she shares with three other dairymaids, one of the girls tells her that Angel Clare is "learning farming in all its branches." His father, the Reverend Mr. Clare of Emminster, is known as the "earnestest man in all Wessex" and all his sons, with the exception of Angel, have become parsons, too.

Commentary

Phase the Third begins by showing us the changes which have taken place in Tess's outlook on life. She has great hopes for the future and she "wishes to walk uprightly." "The irresistible, universal, automatic tendency to find sweet pleasure somewhere, which pervades all life...had at length mastered Tess." Notice how all the descriptive passages intensify what the author has said about Tess. How could her spirits help but rise "on a thyme-scented, bird-hatching morning in May?" The valley to which she comes is "drawn to a larger pattern," the aspect is more cheerful, the air is "clear, bracing, ethereal," the river waters are "clear as the pure River of Life shown to the Evangelist." The contrast between these new surroundings and her past environment sets the scene for Tess's rally.

This is a good chapter to illustrate Hardy's imaginative style. He employs interesting and unusual similes: "She stood still upon the hemmed expanse of verdant flatness like a fly on a billiard-table of indefinite length"; and the cows' "large-veined udders hung ponderous as sandbags, the teats sticking out like the legs of a gipsy's crock." Allusions are made to the Bible, the Greeks, Romans, and Egyptians, as well as to insignificant painters. The dairy is given a timeless quality by phrases, such as "wooden posts rubbed to a glossy smoothness by the flanks of infinite cows and calves of bygone years, now passed to an oblivion almost inconceivable in its profundity."

There is not much humor in this novel; much of what there is can be found in anecdotes such as the one related in Chapter 17.

Angel Clare is seen again as an intruder in the country life. He stands out from his colleagues. Beneath the livery he wears in common with them, there is "something educated, reserved, subtle, sad, differing." He is addressed as "sir" and the dairymaids recognize him as a gentleman.

CHAPTER 18

Summary

Angel Clare is the youngest child of a poor parson. As a youth he showed great promise, yet of the three sons he is the only one not to attend the university. Because of his father's view of advanced education as preparation only for the ministry, Angel believed he would be doing his parents a disservice by attending Cambridge. He has decided he cannot become a minister of a faith to which he cannot wholeheartedly subscribe.

As a result of this decision, his life for the next few years had no direction. He became indifferent to social conventions and scorned "material distinctions of rank and wealth." He went to London to find a business or profession and became involved briefly with an older woman. He realized that he much preferred country life and decided at last that farming was a "vocation which would probably afford an independence without the sacrifice of what he valued even more than a competency—intellectual liberty."

At twenty-six, then, he is learning the practical aspects of farming so that eventually he may establish himself in the Colonies or at home. As a boarder at the dairy, he keeps to himself at first, but soon prefers to eat with the other hands and takes a real delight in their companionship. He begins to appreciate them as individuals. He becomes more aware of nature in all its aspects and as he discovers the joys of outdoor life, he is freed from his formerly persistent melancholy.

Angel's attention is drawn to Tess after several days and his first impression is, "What a fresh and virginal daughter of Nature that milkmaid is!" She seems vaguely familiar to him, a feeling which causes him to choose her when he wishes to look at a pretty girl.

Commentary

The reader's attention is drawn to Angel in this chapter, and we are given a brief summary of his life *as it will affect Tess*. His decision not to enter the ministry and to learn farming has brought him to the dairy—not as an apprentice but as a gentleman learning the practical aspects of the business. He is treated differently from the regular employees. Only when he chooses does he take his meals with the others and even then, Mrs. Crick doesn't feel it fitting that he eat at the same table with the rest. He is really learning a new life. Instead of accepting the caricature of the peasant "Hodge" he begins to appreciate the individual characteristics of the people around him. He "sees something new in life and humanity," and begins to appreciate natural phenomena.

Reference is made to his brief escapade with an older women in London. No emphasis is placed on this affair, but as the reader will see, this becomes a factor in the future relationship of Angel and Tess.

Other aspects of his past which we need to know are his reactions to "good old families" and his relationship with his father who is epitomized as a man of fixed ideas.

Angel's reaction to Tess is ironic. Whereas the first time he saw her he thought of her as pretty, modest, expressive, and soft, this time he thinks of her only as a "fresh and virginal daughter of Nature."

Article 4, one of thirty-nine Articles of Religion of the Church of England, deals with the resurrection of Christ. "Christ did truly rise again from death, and took again his body, with flesh, bones, and all things appertaining to the perfection of Man's nature; wherewith he ascended into Heaven, and there sitteth, until he return to judge all Men at the last day." In order to become a minister of the Church of England, one must swear by all the Articles.

CHAPTERS 19, 20

Summary

Tess soon discovers that her favorite cows are being lined up for her by Mr. Clare, contrary to the dairyman's rules. She tells him of her discovery and then regrets that she has spoken. That evening she walks alone in the garden to continue her misgivings and hears Angel strumming on his harp. He joins her shortly and their conversation sharpens the interest of each for the other. To Angel it is "impressive, interesting and pathetic" that such a young girl should have a somber and pessimistic view of life. To Tess, on the other hand, it is surprising that a "decidedly bookish, musical, thinking young man should have chosen deliberately to be a farmer, and not a clergyman, like his father and brothers."

Tess is depressed when she realizes the difference in learning between them. When Angel offers to teach her, she turns him down by saying that she doesn't want to learn that she is like someone who has gone before her. She would be interested in learning why the sun shines "on the just and the unjust alike" but books will not tell her that.

Tess is anxious to have Angel think highly of her and asks Mr. Crick what Mr. Clare thinks of old families. She learns to her dismay that Angel hates old families because their skills have been used up years ago.

As the season develops Tess and Angel meet continually and become more interested in each other. Tess is happier than she has ever been in her life. She is perfectly suited to her new surroundings and her relationship with Clare is so far one of happy companionship.

Commentary

The choice of Angel's instrument is used by Hardy to add to the picture Tess has of Angel as a god. His amateur playing sounds to her like celestial music and makes her forget her gloomy view of life. She seems "to regard Angel Clare as an intelligence rather than as a man."

But to this picture of incipient love Hardy brings imagery of the most grotesque sort. In the one paragraph description of the garden in which she walks, the author uses "damp," "rank," "offensive smells," "cuckoo-spittle," "snails," "thistle-milk," and "slug-slime." The imagery is an antithesis to the happiness supposedly described, as though the author were warning the reader that it will be an ill-fated love affair.

The importance of the individual is stressed in this book, and Tess's speech in Chapter 19 emphasizes her concern with her own individuality. She considers her own thoughts and actions important and is reluctant to find herself repeated throughout the pages of history and in the time to come.

Angel's offer to teach her anything in the way of history shows that he is ready to make her over, to remold her to fit his die. He finds it difficult to believe that one so young could think original thoughts such as those expressed by Tess. We wonder what he would think if he knew of Tess's experience and how it has changed her life.

Hardy's love of the rural life and the countryside can be gleaned from the descriptions in Chapter 20. The strength that can be derived from close contact with nature brings to Tess more happiness that she has ever known.

Note that the author tells us the lives of Tess and Angel are "converging under an irresistible law, as surely as two streams in one vale." By so doing, he makes the reader more aware of the futility of the struggle on the part of both to keep from being swept together.

As Angel looks at Tess in the predawn hours, he sees her not as an individual, but as "a visionary essence of woman." It is important to remember Angel's idealization of Tess; it will help to explain his reaction when he learns she is mortal.

CHAPTERS 21, 22

Summary

One morning when the butter would not come in the churn, Mr. Crick tells his employees of an earlier time when butter would not come because of damage done to the churn. It is a humorous story to all but Tess who is reminded of her own misfortune. That evening she overhears her companions speak of their love for Angel Clare. She wonders if it is right for her to monopolize his attentions when she has decided never to marry.

The next morning all the hands are set to work in a field trying to find the garlic weeds which have affected the taste of the dairy's butter. Dairyman Crick encourages Tess to leave the work after a while if she should feel faint. Angel drops back with her, and Tess has the opportunity of pointing out the virtues of two of the other milkmaids. After this she takes pains to avoid him, trying to give the other three every chance. She respects his self-disciplined conduct toward all the girls who love him. She had never expected to find this quality in a man.

Commentary

Again the setting changes to conform with the action. Tess sees the sorrow in the story about Jack Dollop, for she can see herself in the shoes of the wronged maiden. "The evening sun was now ugly to her, like a great inflamed wound in the sky." Tess's "wound" has been reopened; it had not been forgotten, but in the benevolent atmosphere of the dairy it was healing.

Tess does not downgrade her opinion of herself. She knows that she is "more finely formed, better educated and...more woman than either" of the dairymaids. She knows there is a slight possibility that Angel Clare might decide a farmwoman would make a good wife. She has decided she can never marry and worries about drawing his attentions to herself when the other girls might be enjoying his companionship. She heroically tries to point out the virtues of the others and obscure her own charms.

The relationship between Angel and Tess is shown in every phase of its development, primarily from Tess's point of view. Contrast this with the summary of Tess's relationship with Alec.

Angel "communistically" takes part with the rest in everything—he is always the gentleman condescending to be a farmer.

CHAPTERS 23, 24

Summary

Two months after her arrival at Talbothays, Tess sets off with the other girls on her first excursion. Dressed in their Sunday best, the girls begin their walk to the Mellstock Church. On the way they find the lane is flooded for about fifty yards as a result of the previous day's heavy rains. Angel, who is out surveying damage to the hay, sees their predicament and offers to carry them through the water. Each of the girls is excited by this unexpected chance to be close to Angel. When Tess's turn comes, he says to her, "Three Leahs to get one Rachel." He takes as long as possible to traverse the pool, then sets her down with the rest and takes his leave. The other girls notice the difference in his attitude toward Tess and fatalistically accept the fact that Angel likes Tess best. That night the girls are depressed, but Tess assures them she doesn't think Angel intends to marry any of them and that she would refuse him if he were to ask her. The girls then tell Tess about the girl Angel's parents want him to marry.

As the heat of July increases, Angel is troubled by his growing feeling for the "soft and silent" Tess. On one afternoon Angel and Tess are milking a few cows who have separated from the rest of the herd. Angel watches Tess and suddenly he goes to her and embraces her. She responds to him unhesitatingly for a moment and then as she realizes the position she is in, she tries to withdraw. Angel tells her he loves her, but is as surprised as Tess at what has just happened. No one has seen what has happened and in a moment they both return to their milking.

Commentary

The three dairymaids are minor characters in this novel, but they serve an important function in emphasizing Tess's personality. By showing their similarities with Tess, the author can picture the Wessex rustic at home in her surroundings, happy in her work, gaining simple pleasures from the life which suits her. By pointing out how Tess differs from the other girls, Hardy stresses the individuality of his heroine and those qualities which make her a memorable character in literature.

The three girls frankly admit they are in love with Angel, but there is no enmity or malice between them as they realize that Angel prefers Tess. Fate has determined this, not Tess. But nevertheless they struggle with their hopeless passion; "the full recognition of the futility of their infatuation... imparts to them a resignation, a dignity, which a practical and sordid expectation of winning him as a husband would have destroyed." Their unrequited love is caricatured somewhat by the author for the humorous effect.

Tess realizes that she, too, loves Angel, "perhaps all the more passionately from knowing that the others have also lost their heart to him." But when she learns that there is a young woman picked out for Angel, she decides his attentions to her are no more than a passing summer romance. She knows that she is "more impassioned in nature, cleverer, more beautiful" than the other girls, but she is also aware that she is "far less worthy of him than the homlier ones." She realizes her predicament only a moment after joyfully yielding to Angel's embrace.

Angel's impulsive nature is shown clearly in Chapter 24. He gazes at her beauty as she is milking, and suddenly "resolutions, reticences, prudences, fears, fall back like a defeated battalion." He gives a "curious sigh of desperation signifying unconsciously that his heart has outrun his judgment" as he tells her he loves her.

Phase the Third ends with Angel's avowal of love. From that point on, the "pivot of the universe" has changed for these two young people and Tess's life once again takes on a new perspective.

PHASE THE FOURTH: THE CONSEQUENCE

CHAPTERS 25, 26

Summary

That evening, Angel contemplates the events of the day and tries to put into perspective his relationship with Tess, the dairy, and his changing view of the future. He feels a great responsibility not to harm Tess's life, which is as precious to her as any person's. So difficult to carry out is his resolve not to approach her that he decides to go away for a few days to visit his family and friends.

Angel finds the family at the breakfast table when he arrives with no advance warning at his father's vicarage at Emminster. Greeting him are his mother and father; his brother, the Reverend Felix, a curate at a town in the adjoining county; and his brother, the Reverend Cuthbert, the classical scholar and Fellow and Dean of his College at Cambridge.

Angel is conscious of the difference in his views regarding life from those of the rest of the family. On their part, his brothers notice quite a change in Angel, especially in his manners, which are now more those of a farmer than of a scholar. As Angel talks to his well-educated and conventional brothers, he notices their growing mental limitations. He believes he sees life much more clearly as it really is lived than either Felix, who seems to him all Church, or Cuthbert, who seems all College.

After the evening prayers Angel and his father discuss the young man's future. The elder Mr. Clare informs Angel that the money he would have spent to send him to Cambridge may be used for the purchase or lease of land. The conversation then turns to the type of wife best suited to the farming life that Angel intends to follow. Angel puts forth the advantages of a woman well versed in farming ways, while Mr. Clare's major interest is in the Christian faith of the woman and he strongly supports the choice of Mercy Chant, the daughter of his friend and neighbor. His mother asks if the woman he has in mind is a lady, coming from the sort of family he would care to marry into. But Angel downgrades social standing and accomplishments, believing these to be of minor importance in a farmer's wife. He waxes quite earnest on the orthodoxy of his beloved Tess, stressing this trait above the others. This aspect of her personality impresses the older couple, who advise Angel not to act in a hurry but say they would not object to seeing her.

On the morning of his departure, Angel's father accompanies him for a little way. The father relates some of his parish difficulties as well as accounts of wonderous conversions he has been responsible for. He also candidly admits many failures, one of whom is a young d'Urberville, in the neighborhood of Trantridge. Mr. Clare had spoken boldly to the delinquent on his spiritual state, which prompted a heated argument. Mr. Clare continues to pray for d'Urberville and hopes his words may have a beneficial influence some day.

Commentary

By having Angel return to his family at this point, the author shows us how his views have changed from those of his family. His mother and father are God-fearing and self-sacrificing with a singleness of purpose which is admirable, but which Angel cannot follow. His brothers are described as "nonevangelical, well-educated, hallmarked young men, correct to their remotest fibre." But to Angel it appears that their vision is very limited, their understanding is confined to their very narrow worlds and the people they meet, and neither can distinguish between a local truth and a universal one.

Although Angel disagrees with some of his father's principles, he admires his father's adherence to them. He wishes not to offend his parents by his choice of wife and finds himself emphasizing qualities in Tess which are not those which attracted him to her. He appreciates his father's unworldliness in not worrying what kind of a family Tess comes from (in contrast to his mother) nor whether she has money or not. We see that Angel means to change Tess somewhat; he feels that she will be open to suggestion regarding her religious convictions and he plans to prescribe her reading for her.

In the ironic discussion about Alec d'Urberville, we discover that Angel has an intense interest in old families and is "lyrically, dramatically and even historically,...tenderly attached to them." The first mention is made here of the ghostly legend of the coach-and-four.

CHAPTERS 27, 28

Summary

Angel returns to the dairy in mid-afternoon when most of the hands are away or taking a nap. He sees Tess as she sleepily comes down from her nap and embraces her. Helping her with the skimming, Angel asks Tess to be his wife. She tells him she cannot marry him, although she loves him and is promised to no one else. He promises to give her time and noticing her distress, he begins to talk generally of his parents and the incidents of his visit. He tells Tess of the encounter between his father and Alec d'Urberville. When he asks her again about his earlier question, she replies hopelessly, "It *can't* be!"

Undaunted, Angel continues to pursue Tess. Thinking that she deems herself unworthy of him, he praises her versatility and her readiness to learn from him. Tess wants him to continue his words of love to her, but she keeps telling him she ought not to marry him. Afraid that she will break her resolve never to marry, Tess unwittingly leads Angel on. At last she tells him she will tell him all about her experiences on Sunday. Tess realizes that her conscience will not be able to hold out against the power of her love for Angel.

Commentary

Angel's impulsive nature is shown in Chapter 27. As he returns to the dairy from a visit to his home, it "affected him like throwing off splints and bandages." Within a few minutes of seeing Tess, he is asking her to marry him "without quite meaning himself to do it so soon." As Tess yawns, Angel sees the red interior of her mouth as if it had been a snake's. This fascinating and grotesque imagery puts the reader on guard concerning Angel's love for Tess.

Angel is pleased with Tess's ability to learn from him, "her natural quickness, and her admiration for him, having led her to pick up his vocabulary, his accent, and fragments of his knowledge, to a surprising extent." Although he professes to want a wife who is able to help manage a farm, he shows that he plans to remold her into the lady and the type of Christian that would please his parents.

"Positive pain and positive pleasure" constitute Tess's life at this point. She loves Angel deeply and is filled with joy whenever Angel speaks of his love for her. She wishes it could go on this way forever, without having to think about marriage. She feels her vow never to marry is the right thing to do, and believes that to marry without telling her husband of her past life would be wrong. But she cannot bear the thought of anyone else having Angel, and Tess realizes that her love will prevail.

CHAPTERS 29, 30

Summary

At breakfast on Sunday morning Dairyman Crick tells the group that Jack Dollop had married a widow for her money, only to find that the income ceased once she was married. The ensuing discussion about whether the woman should have told him before the wedding is amusing to all but Tess. The tale gives her the strength to refuse Angel once more.

Angel does not repeat his proposal for two or three weeks, but continues to woo Tess whenever they meet. One morning in late September Angel insists that she give him an answer. Tess asks him to wait a little and for the last time she tells Angel "perhaps" one of the other girls would make a more proper wife than she.

That evening she goes with Angel to take the milk to the station. Along the way Angel points out an old mansion which formerly belonged to the d'Urberville family. Angel pleads with Tess to become his wife and Tess says she wants to tell him about herself. She tells him a little of her childhood; then, at the last moment, she tells him she is really a descendant of the d'Urbervilles. Angel is surprised at the news, but immediately sees how this will help his mother, and society, accept Tess more readily as his wife. She at last says yes and immediately begins to sob. After kissing Angel passionately, she asks if she may write to her mother. When Angel learns she lives in Marlott he realizes where he has seen Tess before. Tess hopes that Angel's not dancing with her then is not an ill omen for them now.

Commentary

Tess's dilemma whether to tell Angel the truth and risk losing him or to snatch her chance at happiness is complicated by the seemingly innocuous story of Jack Dollop's marriage. It is an amusing discussion to all but Tess; it epitomizes her problem. Although she refuses Angel once more, she knows that in the end she must accept his proposal. "She loves him so passionately, and he is so godlike in her eyes, and being, though untrained, instinctively refined, her nature cries for his tutelary guidance." His manner is "so much that of one who would love and cherish and defend her under any conditions, changes, charges, or revelations, that her gloom lessens as she basks in it." Her "appetite for joy" has overcome her hesitations.

Angel is delighted with the news that Tess is really a d'Urberville. He is certain this will make Tess more acceptable in the eyes of society "after he has made her the well-read woman that he means to make her."

CHAPTERS 31, 32

Summary

Joan answers Tess's letter by advising her not to tell her young man of her former troubles. The responsibility thus shifted from her shoulders, Tess blissfully enjoys her betrothal during the month of October. One night Angel asks Tess to name the day of their wedding, but Tess would like to continue as they are. Angel announces to Dairyman Crick and the maids that they are betrothed. Seeing the girls' astonished reaction, Tess feels again that she is not worthy of Angel's love. She resolves again to tell Angel her history.

During the winter months, few female hands are needed at the dairy, and it is this fact which finally forces Tess's hand. Knowing that she must leave the dairy around Christmas time, she agrees to leave with Angel as his wife. The opportunity arises for Angel to learn the workings of a flour-mill with lodging available in a former mansion of a branch of the d'Urberville family. They decide to go there for a fortnight following their wedding which is set for December 31. Angel takes out a license for the wedding rather than the more usual publication of banns. This is a relief to Tess but she fears she will pay for her good fortune. Angel thoughtfully provides Tess with a complete wedding outfit.

Commentary

The completeness of Tess's love for Angel is shown in these chapters. "There was hardly a touch of earth in her love for Clare. To her sublime trustfulness he was all that goodness could be — knew all that a guide, philosopher, and friend should know. She thought every line in the contour of his person the perfection of masculine beauty, his soul the soul of a saint, his intellect that of a seer." She feels she is not worthy of his love and admiration and yet fears that she might lose him.

Angel's love for Tess tends to be "imaginative and ethereal" and we see that he plans to remold Tess quite extensively. He does not want to leave her for any length of time for fear she will "slip back again out of accord with him," for she has caught "his manner and habits, his speech and phrases, his likings and his aversions." He hopes that a couple of months with him will sufficiently prepare her for her presentation at the Vicarage. And the trump card will be her d'Urberville ancestry.

Angel's decision to spend their honeymoon at the old d'Urberville mansion is a most unfortunate one. The author tells us "this is always how Clare settles practical questions; by a sentiment which has nothing to do with them." Angel is "far from seeing his future track clearly" and realizes that he will not be established for another year or two. He is not ready to publicly announce his intention to wed, for he asks the Cricks to keep secret the date of the wedding and does not publish the banns. So we see some hesitation on his part about the marriage.

CHAPTER 33

Summary

In order to spend a day alone with Tess before they are married, Angel takes her to the nearest town on Christmas Eve to do some shopping. That evening, while Tess is waiting for Angel in the entry of an inn, she is recognized by a Trantridge man who casts doubt on her virginity. Angel overhears his remark and impulsively strikes the man. The man apologizes, Angel gives him five shillings "to plaster the blow," and they part peacefully. Tess is grave on the way home, but she thinks that such occurrences will not happen when they are hundreds of miles away. That night Tess overhears Angel reliving the fight in his sleep and she knows she must confess to Angel. She writes down her troubling experiences, seals the envelope, and slips it under the door of Angel's room. The next morning she sees no change in Angel's attitude toward her and so the next few days pass by.

On the morning of the wedding, the Cricks have decorated the kitchen in their honor. Tess leaves the breakfast table before Angel has finished and hurries to his room. There she finds her letter which has slipped under the carpet, unseen by Angel. Preparations are in full swing for the wedding and she feels she cannot show it to him now, so she destroys it. But she tells him she wants to "confess all her faults and blunders." Angel assures her they both have plenty of time to discuss their failings and that he doesn't want to spoil the day with them.

Mr. and Mrs. Crick accompany them to the church, where they are married in a quiet service. On leaving the church Tess is struck by the familiarity of their carriage, which Angel suggests reminds her of the d'Urberville Coach. As they are leaving the dairy in the early afternoon Tess asks Angel to kiss the three dairymaids good-bye. He shakes hands with the Cricks and just as they are about to leave a cock crows straight toward Clare.

Commentary

To simple and honest Tess, it is not right to marry a man under false pretenses, and she makes her last two attempts to confess to Angel before she is married. In one of the most memorable fatalistic occurrences of the book, her letter slips beneath the carpet and consequently is never seen by Angel. She then tries to tell him but he assures her that the time is not right and that they will *both* confess their failings at a later time.

Angel is a little upset that his family could not attend his wedding, although now he will be able to train Tess for a couple of months before he presents her as his wife. Then he shall "triumphantly" produce her as a d'Urberville and a lady. The author suggests, "perhaps Tess's lineage had more value for himself than for anybody in the world besides." Angel tells her a little of the legend of the d'Urberville Coach.

Tess idolizes Angel to the point that she prays to him instead of to God, and whispers "she you love is not my real self, but one in my image; the one I might have been!" This is indeed the case as the reader will see shortly. Angel does not realize the "full depth of her devotion, its single-mindedness, its meekness; what long-suffering it guarantees, what honesty, what endurance, what good faith." All these adjectives will prove to be accurate in the months ahead.

There is a very old superstition that a cock crowing in the afternoon signifies impending evil.

CHAPTER 34

Summary

Upon arriving at the former d'Urberville mansion, they learn that the farmer has gone away for a few days and they will be alone. As the day ends, a messenger brings a package addressed to "Mrs. Angel Clare." In it is a note from Angel's father reminding Angel that his godmother years ago had bequeathed his wife-to-be some diamonds as a mark of her affection and faith in Angel. Tess puts them on and Angel admires her beauty. At last Jonathan arrives with their luggage and explains that trouble at the dairy accounts for his tardiness. The three dairymaids have not been themselves since the couple left; Retty has tried to drown herself and Marian was found dead drunk.

When they are alone, Angel sits beside Tess and tells her he has something to confess and asks her forgiveness. He tells her about his affair with a woman in London. When he has finished Tess says that she, too, has something to confess and it is just the same as his. She begins her story about Alec d'Urberville.

Commentary

Angel regrets his unfortunate choice of the d'Urberville mansion as he sees the depressing effect it has on Tess. Tess is especially upset by two life-size portraits of her ancestors on panels built into the wall on the landing. Tess's features are discernible in the pictures, which seem to symbolize the treachery and arrogance of her old family.

The reaction of the dairymaids following their departure prove to Tess that she deserves worse at the hands of Fate. "It was wicked of her to take all without paying. She would pay to the uttermost farthing; she would tell, there and then." Tess's guilt at being the chosen one is intensified by these "simple and innocent" girls.

Angel reflects on his responsibility to Tess and hopes that he shall never "neglect her or hurt her or even forget to consider her." But within a few hours he shall do all of these. In his confession to her he emphasizes his belief in good morals and his admiration for purity to which he cannot lay claim. He asks for and receives her forgiveness and then wants to forget the matter completely.

Tess can scarcely believe Angel's words when he tells her he wanted to confess before they were married but dared not risk losing her and hopes that she will not be angry with him for not telling her before. This is exactly her situation! And his confession consists of exactly the type of action she must tell him. She is glad that he has sinned for now he can forgive her. Her crime cannot be more serious then his "because 'tis just the same."

But as she begins her confession the author lets us know, again by grotesque imagery, that it will not be the same. The ashes are like a "torrid waste;" the diamonds on her neck give a "sinister wink like a toad's." Phase the Fourth ends on this note.

PHASE THE FIFTH: THE WOMAN PAYS

CHAPTERS 35, 36, 37

Summary

Angel is devastated by her disclosure. Tess is simply not the woman he has been loving but "another woman in her shape." Tess is terrified by his reaction and begs for his forgiveness. Tess tells him she shall do anything he asks of her, "even if it is to lie down and die." Angel cannot think and goes out of the house. Tess follows him and for hours they walk slowly, Tess occasionally pleading her case. Tess offers to drown herself in the river but Angel asks her not to be absurd and to return to the house and go to bed. This she does and shortly she falls to sleep. When Angel returns to the house he makes his bed on the couch downstairs and goes to the door of her room where he hears her breathing. He is about to leave, turns toward her door again and catches sight of the d'Urberville ladies. He goes downstairs and goes to bed.

In the morning Clare asks Tess to tell him it isn't true, but she cannot lie to him. She tells him the man is still alive and in England. Tess thinks there is a way out by means of divorce, but Angel tells her that is not a possibility. After a somewhat awkward breakfast, Angel goes out to pursue his plan to study the workings of the mill. He returns for meals and spends most of the evening with his papers. And so pass a day or two — Angel trying to think what they must do while hope dies in Tess that they can overcome this breach. On the third day, Tess suggests that she go home and Angel readily agrees.

That night Angel, walking in his sleep, comes into Tess's room, moaning "Dead! Dead! Dead!" wraps her in a sheet, and carries her to the old Abbey church on the grounds and lays her in an empty stone coffin. Tess gently leads him back to the house and to his bed. She does not mention it the next morning and Angel shows no sign of recollection. They stop at the dairy on their way to Marlott. Keeping their estrangement a secret, Angel finishes his business with Mr. Crick while Tess visits with his wife. Angel takes leave of Tess some distance from her home. He tells her he will try to accept the situation, but until he can come to her she should not come to him. He gives her some money, takes the jewels to a banker for safekeeping, and departs. The vehicle takes Tess toward her home.

40

Commentary

These chapters tell us a great deal about Angel's character. He is a man of principle and within his seemingly flexible nature there is a "hard logical deposit, like a vein of metal in soft loam, which turns the edge of everything that attempted to traverse it." His love for Tess, imaginative and fanciful as we have seen it to be, is for what he thinks she is — a pure daughter of nature. The disclosure that she, like he, has sinned in the past, is more than he can comprehend. What satire! Here he has given up all chances for marrying a woman of wealth and stature to obtain rustic innocence and now he finds that even that has been denied him. As Tess feared, the woman he loved is not Tess but another woman in her shape.

To Tess, whose love for Angel is all-encompassing, the change she sees in Angel's attitude toward her takes away all reason for living. She offers to die, if Angel tells her to, and seriously contemplates suicide several times. Her thought in not doing so is not about herself, but how it would affect him. She is willing to do whatever Angel tells her to do. However, whatever she does is wrong, for as she rightly points out to Angel, "it is in your own mind what you are angry at...it is not in me." For the most part, Tess accepts the situation as her just deserts, and "her mood of long-suffering made his way easy for him."

The influence of the d'Urbervilles is great in these chapters. The family name of former luster which Angel thought would help in making Tess acceptable to his family now becomes a convenient tool to exaggerate the enormity of the situation. We are given the impression that Clare might have entered Tess's room if it had not been for the pictures of the d'Urberville women he sees beside her door.

The reader's credulity is stretched to its limit in the sleepwalking sequence. No amount of "suspension of disbelief" can render this melodramatic scene plausible. But it is comforting to Tess to receive his affection and tenderness, even though he is asleep.

Angel tells Tess that if the man were dead it might make a difference and this statement, as we shall see, is prophetic. He points out to Tess the effect her past might have on their children, an argument which she cannot counter. To give her some hope, he says, "I think of people more kindly when I am away from them."

CHAPTERS 38, 39, 40

Summary

Tess dreads returning to her parents' home and shattering their happy illusion that she is married to a gentleman-farmer. She tearfully tells her mother that her confession to Angel caused him to leave her, whereupon Joan calls her a fool. But she accepts the situation quickly, and offers to break the news to Tess's father. Tess sees that there is no room for her in the bedroom, overhears her father ask if she is really married this time, and decides that she cannot stay there for very long. When a letter arrives from Angel informing her that he has gone North to look at a farm, she uses it as a pretext to leave her parents' home. Giving them the impression that she is going to join her husband, Tess leaves them half of the fifty pounds Angel has given her and departs.

Three weeks after their marriage Angel returns to the parsonage to inform his parents that he is leaving for Brazil without Tess. They are naturally curious about his marriage and surprised and disappointed that they will not meet Tess before he goes. He explains that he will return from Brazil after a year and they shall meet her then. The next morning he deposits the jewels and thirty pounds to be sent to Tess in a few months. He writes to her informing her what he has done and tells her to get in touch with his father in case of emergency.

A visit to the Wellbridge farmhouse is necessary and while he is there, Izz Huett calls. Angel offers to take her where she is now living and en route he tells her that he has separated from Tess and is going to Brazil alone. He asks if she will join him. She agrees to go with him and tells him she loves him. But when Angel asks if she loves him more than Tess, Izz says, "No...no more than she...nobody could love 'ee more than Tess did!... She would have laid down her life for 'ee. I could do no more." These words bring Angel to his senses and he turns the horse toward her lane. They part as friends, despite her disappointment, and he sends encouraging messages to the other girls. He takes the train that night for London and five days later leaves for Brazil.

Commentary

Tess must return to her parents' home friendless and alone while they are still celebrating her fortunate marriage. She tells her mother what she has done, but her pride prevents her from letting the family know the extent of the separation. Her mother accepts the situation with her customary resilience, but her father is concerned about the effect of the news on his comrades. Tess's bounty to them upon leaving compensates for the temporary disgrace and they are convinced that the lovers are reconciled.

Angel, too, must deceive his parents. A good example of the use of irony in conversation takes place when they question Angel about his wife. Almost every word uttered by his parents emphasizes the importance of purity and chastity. The Bible chapter chosen by his well-meaning father touches Angel to the core and their magnanimity in accepting his wife reveals to him anew the devastation he has wrought.

Angel is a slave to custom and conventionality almost as much as are his brothers, despite his supposed independence. He regrets that he did not follow his principles by abandoning Tess as soon as he learned of her family heritage. As we have seen, he instead seized the knowledge as a great opportunity and planned to use it as a trump card when producing her for his family's scrutiny. One of the appeals Brazil has for him at this time is that its customs and mores are different from those of England and perhaps life with Tess will seem possible there. Angel begins to doubt if his actions in regard to Tess were wise. He thinks he would have forgiven her if she had told him sooner, but it is unlikely that it would have made much difference. He fancies himself ready to throw over all social conventions and take Izz to Brazil with him, but her honest declaration regarding Tess's love for him, reminds him of the folly and treachery of his impulse.

Hardy departs from his role as an omniscient observer in this chapter, for he tells us that "Nobody ever was told how Izz spent the dark hours that intervened between Angel Clare's parting from her and her arrival home."

CHAPTERS 41, 42

Summary

During the spring and summer following her departure from her parents' home, Tess finds irregular employment at dairies as an extra hand, and during the harvest she finds plenty of work. But as winter approaches she finds she has to spend the money Clare has left her. Her parents write her for help with necessary repairs to their cottage, and she sends them most of what she has remaining. She has managed to keep secret from them the fact that she is a deserted wife, dependent on her own hands for a living. She is equally reluctant to approach Angel's parents, despite his provision for her needs.

Angel at this time is lying ill of fever in Brazil, having been tormented by the weather and afflicted by other hardships.

In November Tess makes her way toward an upland farm where Marian is now employed and where she hopes to find work for the winter. She is overtaken on the road by the Trantridge man who recognized her at the inn before her marriage. Tess, in anguish, runs from him and enters a woods, where she makes a bed under the trees. She wishes she were dead.

To save herself from unwanted advances from admiring young men, Tess dons her oldest clothes, ties a kerchief around her head, and cuts off her eyebrows. She continues on her way, stopping at each farm to inquire for work. The farm to which Marian has encouraged her to come is the last resort, for she has heard of its stringencies. But she finds nothing else.

Reaching the village of Flintcomb-Ash, she is met by Marian, who questions her about her husband and her appearance. Tess asks that she not question her about Angel and not refer to her as Mrs. Clare while she is there. Marian takes her to the farmhouse where the farmer's wife hires her until Old Lady-Day. She finds lodging in the village and that night writes to her parents, informing them of her new address but telling them nothing of her sorry situation.

Commentary

As winter approaches, Tess begins to lose hope that Angel will forgive her. She thinks about her miserable state, the "injustice, punishment, [and] exaction: which she must endure." Tess wishes for death, and symbolically puts the suffering pheasants out of their misery. The sight of their agony, however, convinces her that her self-sympathy is unfounded. "She was ashamed of herself for her gloom of the night, based on nothing more tangible than a sense of condemnation under an arbitrary law of society which has no foundation in Nature."

The setting around the farm at Flintcomb-Ash contrasts sharply with the fertile fields surrounding the Talbothays dairy where Tess found love. In every way the situation here will be different: the landscape is bleak, the soil obviously stubborn, the work as described by Marian will be hard.

Tess has a faithful friend in Marian, who is eager to help her in every way. Marian cannot understand Tess's plight, but she is sure that "something outside [them] both" is the cause of it; neither of them has any faults.

Tess is eager not to bring disgrace to Angel's name. She has a strong sense of justice and believes what is happening to her is fair, although she is very unhappy.

CHAPTERS 43, 44

Summary

For several weeks Tess and Marian work in a rocky field where their job is to dig up rutabagas, the tops of which have been eaten away by the livestock. Their difficult work continues through the wind and rain, but when the snow comes, they are put to work in the barn. Izz Huett joins them that day. Tess finally meets her employer, who is the Trantridge man she has seen several times before. He criticizes her work, but she assures him she will work longer hours to compensate for her lack of skill. But the work in the barn is even more difficult and after a while Tess must rest. When Izz has to leave from exhaustion, Marian relates to Tess Angel's proposal to take Izz with him to Brazil. Tess decides she must write to him, but that evening she is troubled with doubts about her husband.

She then begins to worry why she has not heard from him and decides to visit the Vicarage to express her concern and perhaps learn about him. On a Sunday morning, two weeks later, almost exactly a year following her marriage, she sets off on the fifteen-mile walk to Emminster. She reaches the Vicarage while everyone is at services and decides to wait until the family has eaten before presenting herself. While walking along the lane, she is overtaken by Angel's brothers and overhears them talking about Angel and his unfortunate marriage. They discover her boots, which she has hidden for her walk home, and take them for some poor person. Feeling condemned by Angel's family, Tess cannot return to the Vicarage and begins her journey home. About half way she hears an evangelical sermon being delivered in a barn by a visiting preacher. Both the words and the voice of the speaker draw Tess to the entrance, where she sees Alec d'Urberville.

Commentary

One of the basic tenets of Hardy's philosophy is expressed in Chapter 43. "So the two forces were at work here as everywhere, the inherent will to enjoy, and the circumstantial will against enjoyment." Even amidst the deprivation and hardship of her surroundings and her present condition, Tess can find happiness in her memories of the Talbothays.

Tess continues to hope that her magnanimous husband will eventually join her. "Patience, that blending of moral courage with physical timidity, is now no longer a minor feature in Mrs. Angel Clare; and it sustains her." She is upheld by the fact that she is his wife, even if in name only.

Note that Tess is not afraid of her employer; she "has nothing to fear from her employer's gallantry." She feels "she could not have come to a much worse place; but anything was better than gallantry." This attitude will be shown again when Alec begins to pay attention to her.

Tess shows again that she wants nothing to which she is not entitled "on a fair consideration of her deserts." She feels she has no claim on Angel's family, just because he impulsively married her. But she does hope that she can win her mother-in-law's sympathies and thereby win back Angel. She makes a tragic mistake in judging Angel's parents by his brothers.

Phase the Fifth ends as Tess once again faces her seducer. Had she followed through on her plan to visit the Clares, she probably would not have seen Alec, and the course of her life would have been altogether different.

PHASE THE SIXTH: THE CONVERT

CHAPTERS 45, 46

Summary

Tess has not seen or heard from d'Urberville since she left Trantridge. As she looks at the convert expressing his regret for his past deeds, a paralyzing fear comes over her. As soon as she starts to leave, Alec recognizes her with a reaction even more intense than Tess's. Alec catches up with her in order to save her soul. He tells Tess that his conversion resulted from an encounter with Mr. Clare. Tess scoffs at his conversion and tells Alec she does not believe in his "scheme of religion" because a better man than he has rejected it. Alec is unnerved by Tess's gaze and asks her to put her veil down. When they come to a stone pillar called "Cross-in-Hand" Alec asks her to swear on it that she will "never tempt him — by [her] charms or ways." Half frightened, Tess so swears. As Alec walks from her he reads a well-worn letter from Mr. Clare and other material until he has regained his composure. Tess asks a shepherd the meaning of the "Cross-in-Hand" and learns that instead of a Holy Cross it is a "thing of ill omen."

A few days later Alec finds Tess in the fields and asks her to marry him and go with him as a missionary in Africa. She tells him she cannot because she is married to another man. Alec is surprised and disappointed and surmises that Tess is a deserted wife. Tess begs him to leave. Tess tries again to write to Angel but does not finish the letter.

Alec calls on Tess again on the day of the Candlemas Fair. He asks Tess to pray for him, and she answers, "How can I pray for you...when I am forbidden to believe that the great Power who moves the world would alter His plans on my account?" Tess tells Alec she does have a religion but doesn't believe in anything supernatural. She recites Angel's arguments, which have an unsettling effect upon Alec. He tells her he has canceled an appointment to preach in order to see her again. He is upset by the fact that he has no legal right to protect her while the man who does seems to neglect her. His passion for her has returned. She implores him to be ashamed and to leave before any scandal should touch her husband's name.

Commentary

The author has not prepared the reader for the sight of Alec as a repentant sinner. Nothing has been heard about him other than his tussle with Mr. Clare. Tess is extremely skeptical of his sudden reformation. The author intensifies this reaction by his interesting description of the "new" Alec. Each aspect of his appearance is compared and slightly contrasted to his look of old. "The lineaments, as such, seemed to complain. They had been diverted from their hereditary connotation to signify impressions for which nature did not intend them." Tess is struck, too, by the irony of the situation. She is indignant with men like Alec who "take [their] fill of pleasure on earth by making the life of such as [her] bitter and black with sorrow; and then it is a fine thing, when [they] have had enough of that, to think of securing [their] pleasure in heaven by becoming converted."

Tess becomes "the innocent means of [Alec's] backsliding." By her ability to parrot Angel's arguments regarding religion, she unwittingly shows Alec that his position is untenable. "The drops of logic Tess has let fall into the sea of his enthusiasm serve to chill its effervescence to stagnation." Just the sight of her face is enough to revitalize Alec's passion for her.

Tess takes very seriously her responsibility to protect Angel's honor. She will not allow a word to be said against him and begs Alec to leave her "before any scandal spreads that may do harm to his honest name." She believes that Angel knows everything and is willing to accept his beliefs, which are based on study and research.

Even Alec looks upon Tess as being "unsmirched in spite of all" because she "withdrew [herself] from [him] so quickly and resolutely when [she] saw the situation; [she] did not remain at [his] pleasure." He accepts all the blame for their affair and feels somewhat responsible for her present state. He is astonished that she has married someone else and ironically asks, "but has not a sense of what is morally right and proper any weight with you?"

CHAPTERS 47, 48

Summary

In March Alec appears at the farm no longer dressed as a preacher. He joins Tess on the threshing machine while she eats her lunch and tells her he is no longer a preacher. He is more in love with her than ever and he pities her because she is neglected by one who ought to cherish her. He asks her to come away with him. "You have been the cause of my back-sliding...you should be willing to share it, and leave that mule you call husband for ever." Tess picks up one of her leather gloves and swings it across his face. Angrily Alec seizes her by the shoulders and tells her, "Remember, my lady, I was your master once! I will be your master again. If you are any man's wife you are mine!" Alec leaves her, saying he will return for her answer during the afternoon.

Tess continues the exhausting and difficult work to which she has been assigned. When the threshing is finally completed, Alec is there beside her to walk her home. He asks her to trust him. He has the means to take care of her and her family. Tess tells him she will accept nothing from him, either for herself or her family.

That night she writes a passionate letter to Angel telling him of her devotion to him and of the temptation which confronts her and begging him to come back to her.

Commentary

Several aspects of Tess's relationship with Alec are shown again. Her temper can be aroused by him, this time by an insult to her beloved husband, and she strikes back physically. The power which Alec holds over Tess is through his provision for her family. We see here a momentary hesitation when he offers to take care of them. She at first says to help them without telling her about it, but then quickly changes to a complete refusal of his offer.

Alec tells Tess, "ever since you told me of that child of ours, it is just as if my feelings, which have been flowing in a strong puritanical stream, had suddenly found a way open in the direction of you, and had all at once gushed through. The religious channel is left dry forthwith; and it is you who have done it!" Alec vacillates between a sincere desire to help Tess and a wish to master her again. He blames her for his backsliding and he wants her to share the results. He cunningly takes advantage of Tess's weakened and confused state brought about by privation and physical fatigue.

CHAPTERS 49, 50

Summary

The letter is sent to the Vicarage and is promptly redirected to Angel. Mrs. Clare tells her husband that Angel should have had the opportunity of going to Cambridge despite his want of faith. Mr. Clare feels justified in his decision, but laments for his beloved Angel; "his silent, self-generated regrets" are far more bitter than the reproaches of his wife.

Angel by this time has almost decided to give up his hopes of farming in Brazil. He has aged mentally a great deal since coming to this disillusioning land, and has reappraised his thoughts on morality. Angel confides the story of his marriage to another Englishman, a man who has lived in many more lands and among many more people than Angel. He views the matter quite differently and plainly tells Clare that he was wrong to leave Tess. Within a few days, the stranger is laid low by fever and dies. The words of this man affect Clare deeply, and he is struck with remorse as he realizes the inconsistencies of his thinking. "Thus from being [Tess's] critic he grows to be her advocate." Love is reborn, paving the way for Tess's devoted outpouring, which is on its way to him.

One evening, when her term at the farm is almost completed, Tess is startled by the appearance of her sister, 'Lisa-Lu. The latter bears the news that their mother is very ill, on the verge of death, and their father, also ill, refuses to work. Tess decides to go at once, and arranges for her sister to spend the night at the cottage and to follow her the next morning. She tells Izz and Marian the situation and asks them to explain as best they can to the farmer.

Tess pursues the shortest route home, a walk of some fifteen miles. The next few days are spent nursing her mother, caring for the family and the indoor necessities. When her mother's health improves sufficiently, Tess turns her attention to planting and sowing the family garden and working on their plot just outside the village.

One night as she is working by the light of the fire burning the grasses which she removes from the plot, she is startled to see Alec working alongside her. Alec again offers to help her and her family. Although Tess would like to ease the lives of her brothers and sisters, she feels it is not right to accept help from Alec. He becomes angry and leaves.

On the way home, Tess is met by one of her sisters bearing the grim news that their father is dead. This means the loss of the family house, for

John Durbeyfield's life was the last for whose duration the house and premises were held under a lease. It has long been coveted by the tenant farmer for his own laborers.

Commentary

Important changes have taken place in Angel's thinking, preparing the way for a reconciliation. Angel is very like his father in his adherence to principles. But while he was able to liberate his mind from his father's narrow religious views, he was unable to free himself from the constraints of social convention. His experiences in a foreign land and especially his encounter with a dying cosmopolitan stranger broaden his vision and enable him to accept Tess. "The beauty or ugliness of a character [lies], not only in its achievements, but in its aims and impulses," he decides; "its true history [lies], not among things done, but among things willed." When he views Tess in these lights, a regret for his hasty judgment begins to oppress him.

The author reminds us that "flux and reflux—the rhythm of change—alternate and persist in everything under the sky." Probably when the d'Urbervilles were in their glory they turned out many a lease-holder, just as the Durbeyfields are being treated now.

CHAPTERS 51, 52

Summary

On the eve of Old Lady-Day—the day when the laborers change to new farms in the hope of happier employment—Tess sits dejectedly by the window while her mother, 'Liza-Lu and Abraham bid good-bye to friends. Alec rides up and tells Tess the legend of the d'Urberville Coach, which is said to be an ill omen for the one who hears the sound of a nonexistent coach. Tess tells Alec they are going to Kingsbere, where they have taken rooms. Alec generously offers them lodging in the garden house at Trantridge. He says he will send the children to a comfortable school and provide a colony of fowls for Tess's mother to tend. Tess is choked with emotion, but tells Alec they will not come. He wants a chance to repay her a little for the past, but Tess still mistrusts him and tells him she has plenty of money at her father-in-law's. Alec, however, knows she would starve before she would ask for money, and he rides off.

Tess for the first time admits that her husband has treated her unjustly and is filled with self-pity. She passionately writes Angel that she will try to forget him, that she can never forgive him for the monstrous way in which he has treated her. When her mother returns she refuses to tell her what Alec said to her, promising to tell her all when they are settled in their rooms at Kingsbere the next day.

Their household goods are loaded on a hired wagon the next day and they leave Marlott. During one of the rest stops, Tess sees Marian and Izz, who are bound for a new location. They learn from Tess that Alec has found her and that Angel still has not returned. They exchange addresses and bid each other good-bye.

On the outskirts of Kingsbere, they are informed that Joan's letter just arrived that morning and the rooms have already been let. The search for other lodging is unfruitful and when the driver says the goods must be unloaded, Joan recklessly tells him to put them under the churchyard wall. By the part of the church known as d'Urberville Aisle and under the d'Urberville Window they set up a four-post bedstead and make a tent for the youngsters by drawing the curtain around the bed.

While the mother and the two older children seek other lodging and food, Tess wanders into the church and sees for the first time the vaults of her ancestors. Drawing close to an old altar tomb, she is shocked to discover Alec lying there. Alec tells her that he, the sham d'Urberville, can do more for her than the whole dynasty of the real within the vaults. Tess tells him to go away. As he leaves, he whispers, "Mind this; you'll be civil yet!"

When he is gone she bends down upon the entrance to the vaults and says, "Why am I on the wrong side of this door!"

Meanwhile Marian and Izz try to help mend the breach between Tess and Angel. About a month after settling at their new establishment, they write a touching note to Angel at the Emminster Vicarage urging him to look to his wife for she is threatened by an enemy.

Commentary

The legend of the d'Urberville Coach is finally revealed to a degree in Chapter 51. After the number of allusions to it, one would expect it to have more bearing on the story than merely another ill omen. Alec's version is one of several, and he cannot remember all the details. But it gives the reader a clue that Tess will be involved in a murder.

The sign painter appears again briefly. He serves to remind Alec of how far he has strayed from the words of the Scriptures and from his temporary life as a preacher.

Tess wishes she could believe that Providence would bring happiness to her siblings, but she cannot trust them to such an uncertain fate. She feels compelled to be their Providence herself. She feels responsible for the removal of her family from their house, which was theirs as long as her father lived. Her family might have been able to stay on as weekly tenants had she not come home.

Her sense of justice outraged, she finally writes Angel that she cannot forgive him for the cruel way he has treated her. She has been punished severely and persistently for sins of inadvertence, never of intention.

PHASE THE SEVENTH: FULFILMENT

CHAPTERS 53, 54, 55

Summary

Angel's parents are shocked by his appearance when he returns home. Worry, the bad season, and illness have reduced their son to a walking skeleton. So changed is he that they would scarcely have recognized him had they not been expecting him. He asks if any letters have come for him and reads the unforgiving words which Tess expressed in her last hurried note to him. His mother suggests he should not be so anxious about a "mere child of the soil." He replies by telling her for the first time that Tess is a descendant of one of the oldest Norman houses.

Feeling unwell, Angel remains at home the following day, worrying about the possible change in Tess's estimate of him. In an attempt to prepare her for his return, he writes to her in care of her family at Marlott, where he hopes she is still living. Within a week he receives a note from Joan informing him that Tess is not with her and that the family has been away from Marlott for some time.

He waits for a few days for Joan to let him know that Tess has returned, but then decides he must find her immediately. He learns from his father that she has not applied for money during his absence and realizes for the first time that pride stood in her way and that she has suffered privation. His parents deduce from his remarks the real reason for their separation, and Tess's sin excites their tenderness. As he hastily packs for his journey, he reads the poor, plain letter which has arrived from Marian and Izz.

With a feeling of urgency, Angel begins his search for Tess, following the same path by which she had come on her ill-fated journey three or four months earlier. At Flintcomb-Ash he learns of the hardships she has undergone and her dignified sense of their total separation in not using his name. He is told that Tess has returned to the home of her parents.

At Marlott he finds that John Durbeyfield is dead and learns where Joan has gone. In the churchyard he notices the headstone of John Durbeyfield, which is of superior design to the rest and which traces his ancestry to the d'Urbervilles. On learning that this memorial, for all the flourish, is unpaid for he takes care of the bill before continuing his journey.

Joan is embarrassed by his visit and reluctant to tell him where Tess is. Angel pleads with her as a lonely, wretched man, and Joan, seeing that he has suffered, tells him that Tess is at Sandbourne.

Arriving at Sandbourne too late in the evening to inquire for anyone, Angel secures a room and walks the streets for a while. At seven the next morning he goes to the postoffice to try to find a Mrs. Clare, or a Miss Durbeyfield. One of the postmen tells him there is a d'Urberville staying at a stylish lodging house, The Herons. He goes there immediately and as he is ushered into the front room by the landlady he thinks that Tess must have sold the jewels in order to live in such a place, for which he does not blame her at all.

Mrs. d'Urberville, as she is known there, appears at the doorway attired in expensive clothes which make her natural beauty more obvious. Angel holds out his arms, but Tess does not come to him.

"Tess!" he says huskily, "can you forgive me for going away? Can't you — come to me? How do you get to be — like this?"

"It is too late," says she, "her voice sounding hard through the room, her eyes shining unnaturally."

Angel tells her that he has learned to see her as she is, that she must surely love him since he has been sick, that his mother and father will welcome her now. She tells him again it is too late; she has succumbed to Alec's kindnesses and persuasion and he has won her back to him. She says she hates Alec for telling her that Angel would never come back to her, now that he has come. She begs Angel to go away and never return.

They stand fixed, "their baffled hearts looking out of their eyes with a joylessness pitiful to see. Both seem to implore something to shelter them from reality." Tess leaves. In a trance Angel finds himself in the street, going he knows not where.

Commentary

Changes in Angel are emphasized in Chapter 53. His physical appearance has changed considerably; he is very thin, his "sunken eye pits are of morbid hue,...the light in his eyes has waned," and his face looks twenty years older. The change in his regard for Tess has undergone as complete a transformation and he wonders why he has not judged Tess "constructively rather than biographically, by the will rather than by the deed." For the first time he realizes what she must have gone through during their separation.

Angel's parents are presented as loving, forgiving, and kind. What problems might have been averted if Angel's pride had allowed him to discuss with them the reason for the separation.

In Chapter 54 the author again stresses the importance of each person's individual life. The new inhabitants of the Durbeyfield cottage can scarcely remember their predecessors' names and consider their own story every bit as interesting as anyone else's.

The uselessness of John's noble ancestry continues after his death. Even his distinguished headstone is unpaid for. He would have rather taken his place among the ancestors at Kingsbere.

The confrontation of the two lovers is a very moving scene. Who can blame Tess for giving in to Alec after the hard measure Angel exacted from her? Angel is stunned that his loving and forgiving Tess would send him away from her.

Tess has been beaten down by her struggles, adversities, and thwarted hopes to the point where she passively allows Alec to do what he will with her, to clothe her in whatever fashion pleases him.

CHAPTER 56

Summary

The landlady, Mrs. Brooks, is not an unusually curious woman, but the time and manner of Angel's visit to her well-paying tenants are sufficiently unusual to pique her usually repressed curiosity. She follows Tess up the stairs and through the keyhole she sees the despairing woman kneeling in front of a chair, her hands clasped over her head. She overhears Tess blaming Alec for making her believe that Angel would never come back to her, that he has come and now she has lost him again, this time forever. Mrs. Brooks leaves her vantage point as the man answers sharply, for she fears discovery. She enters her own parlor and waits for the call to take the breakfast things away. She sees Tess go out the gate on her way to the street. Pondering the silence above and the situation in general, she leans back in her chair and notices a growing red spot on the ceiling. It is blood. Failing in courage to enter the room alone, she calls a neighboring workman and follows him to the door of the bedroom.

The man opens the doors, enters a step or two, and comes back almost instantly with a rigid face. "My good God, the gentleman in bed is dead! I think he has been hurt with a knife — a lot of blood has run down upon the floor!"

The alarm is soon given and within "a quarter of an hour the news that a gentleman who is a temporary visitor to the town has been stabbed in his bed spreads through every street and villa of the popular watering-place."

Commentary

This is an unusual chapter, for the scene is related as seen by the landlady. Some of the melodramatic aspects are lessened thereby, and it is rendered more believable.

Her character is admirably drawn. We take her to be a woman who is not overly imaginative nor curious; therefore, what she sees must surely be true. If she sees blood dripping through the ceiling, it must be there! Presented in a different manner, this occurrence might be incredible. The similarity between the spot and a gigantic ace of hearts makes the occurrence even more fantastic.

CHAPTERS 57, 58

Summary

Brokenhearted, Angel returns to his hotel, packs, and decides to take the first train out of town. He receives a telegram from his mother as he is leaving which informs him that his brother, Cuthbert, has proposed to and been accepted by Mercy Chant. There is an hour's wait for the train, but after a few minutes he decides to walk to the first station and let the train pick him up there.

As he is climbing out of the valley which lies outside of the town he looks back and sees a figure running after him. It is not until she is quite close that he recognizes his beloved Tess. He does not question her, but leads her off the road and takes a footpath under some fir trees.

"Angel," she says, "do you know what I have been running after you for? To tell you that I have killed him!"

Angel thinks she must be delirious. Tess continues by rationalizing her actions: Alec set a trap for her in her youth and thereby wronged Angel; Tess was obliged to go back to Alec because Angel didn't return to her. She asks Angel to forgive her sin against him now that she has killed Alec and asks him to declare his love for her.

"I do love you, Tess—O, I do—it is all come back!"

Slowly he is "inclined to believe that she has faintly attempted, at least, what she says she has done." Tenderness is absolutely dominant in Clare at last. He kisses her endlessly and tells her he will not desert her, but "will protect [her] by every means in [his] power…whatever [she] may have done."

They continue their walk though the trees, heading more or less north-ward and avoiding the highways. Neither seems to have a plan. Angel buys them food enough to last them for a day or two and decides they should head for the interior of the country until the search might be called off. Then they can head for some port.

Toward evening they come upon an empty mansion whose rooms are aired daily by a woman from a nearby hamlet. They enter through an open window, find a large chamber upstairs, and remain in darkness until the woman comes to close up the house and leaves. Then Clare opens the shutters slightly, they share another meal and are soon "enveloped in the shades of night."

Five days pass by in absolute seclusion. By tacit consent, they hardly speak of the period following their wedding day. Tess is reluctant to leave this place of "affection, union, and error forgiven," for the trouble and the inexorable of the outside world.

On the sixth day, the caretaker arrives early in the morning and dis-covers their hiding place. Although they do not see her, they sense the time has come to move on. Tess knows that her life can only be a question of a few weeks and wishes they could stay in the happy house. But Angel tries to assure her that they can escape by traveling out of Wessex to a port in the north.

That night they come upon the gigantic pillars of Stonehenge. Tess is very tired by this time and lies down upon an oblong slab that is sheltered from the wind by a pillar. Tess says she feels very much at home in a heathen temple, where it seems as if there are no people in the world but them.

Angel covers her with his overcoat and sits down by her side. Tess asks him to watch over 'Liza-Lu after she is gone, and he promises that he will. Tess wishes Angel would marry 'Liza-Lu after she is gone. Her sister has all her good traits and none of the bad, and if Angel married her it would almost seem as if death had not divided them.

Tess asks Angel if he thinks they shall meet again after they are dead. Angel kisses her to avoid a reply. "O, Angel—I fear that means no!" says she, with a suppressed sob. "And I wanted so to see you again—so much, so much! What—not even you and I, Angel, who love each other so well?"

He does not answer, and soon she falls asleep. As day approaches, Angel sees men moving toward them from all directions. They are closing in with evident purpose and he knows then that her story is true. He implores them to let her finish her sleep. She is almost glad they have come for her. Her happiness could not have lasted, and she does not want to live for Angel to despise her.

Commentary

Angel has finally lived up to Tess's estimation of him as protector against all adversaries, no matter what she has done. Tess seems at last content and weeps with happiness at being together with him again.

In Chapter 36 Angel says to Tess, "How can we live together while that man lives?—he being your husband in Nature, and not I. *If he were dead it might be different.*" Knowing how thoroughly Tess retained what Angel taught her, it is not unlikely that she consciously or subconsciously remembered these words. Tess says, "It came to me as a shining light that I should get you back that way." She expects forgiveness of her sin against Angel, and he forgives her. What a different story this would have been if Angel could have forgiven her for her earlier transgression.

Angel still cannot comprehend Tess's love for him. "His horror at her impulse is mixed with amazement at the strength of her affection for him, and at the strangeness of its quality, which has apparently extinguished her moral sense altogether." "There momentarily flashes through his mind that the family tradition of the coach and murder might have arisen because the d'Urbervilles had been known to do these things."

The Stonehenge scene is a memorable one with great sensory effects. Angel and Tess spend their last moments together in a heathen temple, with Tess lying upon an altar which in ancient times might have been used for sacrifices to the sun. As the sun rises, she is sacrificed to the guardians of social law and morals.

We see that Angel has not rid himself entirely of his conventional training when he expresses surprise at the thought of marrying his sister-in-law.

CHAPTER 59

Summary

From a hillside outside the city of Wintoncester Angel and 'Liza-Lu watch the black flag move slowly up the staff on the cornice of the tower. "The two speechless gazers bend themselves down to the earth, as if in prayer, and remain thus a long time, absolutely motionless: the flag continues to wave silently. As soon as they have strength they arise, join hands again, and go on."

" 'Justice' was done, and the President of the Immortals, in Æschylean phrase, has ended his sport with Tess. And the d'Urberville knights and dames sleep on in their tombs unknowing."

Commentary

There is bitter irony in the phrase " 'justice' was done," which intensifies the tragedy of Tess's life. It is a defiant, despairing cry against the injustice of the universal plan.

Prometheus, in *Prometheus Bound* by Æschylus, says,

> Yes, of a surety—though he do me wrong,
> Loading my limbs with fetters strong—
> The president
> Of heaven's high parliament
> Shall need me yet to show
> What new conspiracy with privy blow

Attempts his sceptre and his kingly seat.
Neither shall words with all persuasion sweet,
Not though his tongue drop honey, cheat
Nor charm my knowledge from me; nor duress
Of menace dire, fear of more grievous pains,
Unseal my lips, till he have loosed these chains,
And granted for these injuries redress.

ANALYSIS AND DISCUSSION

TECHNIQUE

Hardy was a craftsman who could take a simple plot and mold it into a living and enduring work of art. Written first as a novel, but then cut for serial publication in a family magazine, *Tess* depended a great deal on sensational incidents to sustain the interest of the readers from one month to the next. Hardy found distasteful the changes necessary to make the novel suitable for a popular magazine. Those sections which might offend the taste or jeopardize the morals of family readers were eliminated as were those passages suggesting skepticism or lack of reverence toward the existing forms of faith. Examples of the changes: the descriptions of the midnight baptism and the Saturday night dance at Chaseborough were eliminated; Tess "thought she had married" Alec, she had no baby, and at the end of the story, she lived near Alec as a "friend."

Hardy objected to the difficult job of remaking his novel for book publication in 1891. In so doing, however, he changed some of the original by improving certain sentences, adding Biblical and literary references to add tone to his writing. For the Wessex Edition of 1895 he added much of the dialect and rustic touches.

Hardy was an independent writer who wanted nothing more than to write honestly and freely, unhampered by limitations of public taste and morality. What at times seems to the modern reader as a great deal of fuss about nothing much, must have appeared to the Victorian reader as shocking indeed. The criticism heaped upon him following the publication of *Tess* and *Jude* finally prompted him to give up novel writing altogether and turn to poetry, where he felt he would write with greater freedom for a smaller and more intelligent audience.

POINT OF VIEW

Hardy is the omniscient narrator of the tale of Tess. He knows everything about her: her secret thoughts, her motives, her feelings about and reaction to people and events. He is definitely her advocate and at many points, he intrudes into the story to explain or justify or comment on her actions. He tells us almost all he knows about Tess.

He does not know all about some of the lesser characters and tells us only what is significant to the story of Tess about any of them.

Much of the story is told in summary narrative form. Only during the idyll of the Talbothays dairy, while the love between Angel and Tess is developing, is there an extended pictorial presentation.

SETTING

The boundaries of Hardy's imaginary Wessex are practically identical with those of the historical Kingdom of the Wessex, which included the present counties of Berkshire, Wilts, Somerset, Hampshire, Dorset, and Devon in the South of England. Hardy has described this area more extensively than any other English writer. His descriptions of roads, valleys, hamlets, villages, towns, woods, meadows, inns, and houses is so realistic that it prompted many fans to research into the actual names of the places mentioned. The names used by Hardy are in many cases changed only slightly from the original.

Wessex, in Hardy's hands, is a dramatically useful device. In this circumscribed world, so familiar to Hardy from boyhood on, the author can focus on the elementary passions of its inhabitants and their closely knit interdependence. The conditions of life Hardy describes are those of his boyhood, when there had been no break in the continuity of memories, habits, and instincts. Many of the difficulties encountered by his character are a result of the intrusion of machines or of people who do not belong. The migrations of workers to new abodes each Old Lady-Day is a scene of tragedy to Hardy, for it means additional loss of customs, folklore, and nomenclature.

The locale of each event in *Tess* is appropriate to the action taking place in it. The description of the setting, and of the season, add depth and deeper meaning to the events unfolding at that time. The most striking example of this is, of course, the period of Tess's recovery of her serenity and happiness in an environment which suggests fertility and a changeless placidity. Her growing love for Angel coincides with the advancing season; every change in their relationship proceeds naturally from some normal event in the life of the dairy. The atmosphere of the dairy is sustained for over one hundred pages, and within it is dramatized Tess's reconstruction and Angel's intrusion in this world of innocence and naturalism with his discordant Victorianism.

As Tess's plight grows more tragic, the weather turns more bitter and the lush, fertile valleys are left behind for the starve-acre land of Flint-comb-Ash. Society and nature have combined forces against her, but her struggle against these almost insurmountable odds brings respect for her courage.

Other examples of the setting fitting the action are numerous and striking. In Chapter 3 Tess returns "from the holiday gaieties of the field – the white gowns, the nosegays, the willow wands, the whirling movements on the green, the flash of gentle sentiment towards the stranger – to the yellow melancholy of this one-candled spectacle, what a step!" A little later she rebukes her mother. "Her rebuke and her mood seemed to fill the whole room, and to impart a cowed look to the furniture, and candle, and children playing about, and to her mother's face."

Nature, as well as material things, takes on a different aspect depending upon the mood or disposition of the onlooker. For example, after hearing the anecdote about Jack Dollop, which amuses the rest of the dairy but strikes too close to Tess's secret for her to see any humor in it, Tess wanders aimlessly outside. "The evening sun was now ugly to her, like a great inflamed wound in the sky" (Chapter 21).

Another notable example is the description of the fire and of Tess wearing the bridal gift of diamonds just before Angel begins his confession: "A steady glare from the now flameless embers painted the sides and back of the fireplace with its colour...the underside of the mantel-shelf was flushed with the high-coloured light...Tess's face and neck reflected the same warmth, which each gem turned into an Aldebaran or a Sirius – a constellation of white, red, and green flashes, that interchanged their hues with her every pulsation."

Tess is ready to begin her confession: "The ashes under the grate were lit by the fire vertically, like a torrid waste. Imagination might have beheld a Last Day luridness in this red-coated glow, which fell on his face and hand, and on hers, peering into the loose hair about her brow, and firing the delicate skin underneath. A large shadow of her shape rose upon the wall and ceiling. She bent forward, at which each diamond on her neck gave a sinister wink like a toad's."

She has finished her confession: "The fire in the grate looked impish — demoniacally funny, as if it did not care in the least about her strait. The fender grinned idly, as if it too did not care. The light from the water-bottle was merely engaged in a chromatic problem. All material objects around announced their irresponsibility with terrible iteration. And yet nothing had changed since the moments when he had been kissing her; or rather, nothing in the substance of things. But the essence of things had changed."

What power and meaning these descriptions bring to the scene! What tragedy they portend.

It is fitting that Angel and Tess must withdraw completely from the world they have known to gain their brief moments of happiness. Society and nature have joined against them in their search for enjoyment.

The law puts an end to their romance among the ancient and awesome monuments of Stonehenge. This is the one setting which seems foreign to the rest of the novel; the author seems to be stretching for a sensational ending and settles for Stonehenge as an ancient heathen temple.

STYLE — LANGUAGE

Hardy's use of language is at the same time one of his weaknesses and that which marks his individuality as an author. His ear for the rustic dialect delighted his contemporaries but it means much less to the modern reader. Many of his phrases are cumbersome and he uses a number of words which are obsolete. On the other hand, his instinct as a poet causes him to use imaginative words and phrases, to color his scenes vividly with all the overtones and subtleties of the mood in which he regards them. He penetrates beneath the material facts to reveal their imaginative significance, and by infusing mystery and magic into his descriptions, he makes them memorable. He is sensitive to rhythm in his prose and can write eloquently and expressively.

GROTESQUE IMAGERY

Hardy makes use of a grotesque imagery to provide the reader with a more penetrating vision. A good example of this may be seen in Chapter 19 where Tess walks in the garden listening to the sound of Angel's music. She is fascinated and draws closer to the performer. Supposedly, this is

62

the beginning of love, but as she walks she gathers cuckoo-spittle on her skirts, cracks snails that are underfoot, stains her hands with thistle-milk and slug-slime, and rubs off upon her naked arms sticky blights. Can this overgrown garden perhaps suggest an impending catastrophe? Surely the images are ironically incongruous with the happiness Hardy is talking about.

Another example may be found in Chapter 27 when Angel sees the inside of Tess's mouth "as if it had been a snake's." In the midst of the Talbothays idyll—the Garden of Eden—there is a hint of evil and betrayal.

This imagery is unexpected, evocative, and effective in bringing to the reader a more significant esthetic experience.

CHARACTER ANALYSES

TESS

The subtitle of *Tess of the d'Urbervilles* reads "A Pure Woman Faithfully Presented," and so she is. Tess is the central character of the book. Her life for a period of some four years is presented in detail; her thoughts about a variety of subjects and her emotions are explored in all their facets. The other characters are presented only as they affect Tess's life. Her growth and development from a simple, country girl to a complex woman weaves throughout the novel, while the changes occurring in the men she knows are presented only summarily. Only two minor characters, those of Angel's parents, never come in contact with Tess. All the others come into the spotlight only when Tess is also on the stage.

Although born of shiftless parents of very limited means, Tess exhibits qualities worthy of her illustrious ancestors. Throughout the novel we are impressed by the nobility of her character, by her pride, loyalty, and honesty. She realizes her importance as an individual and wishes to walk uprightly throughout her life.

Tess if often compared to a "bird caught in a trap," and by the repeated use of this metaphor the author pictures his heroine as almost without blame for her sin against society. The "trap" was set both by her parents and by Alec. She is sent out into the world at a very young age, innocent to the dangers which might await her. Her mother, with visions of a fancy marriage for her pretty daughter, gives little thought to the type of man her daughter will be associated with. Her father, also thinks only of his own desire to restore the family name to its former stature. Alec takes advantage of her innocence and physical exhaustion to seduce her.

Tess has a strong moral sense as well as a keen awareness of justice. She realizes she has sinned, but she does not feel she should be punished eternally for one mistake. The other girls at the dairy constantly serve to remind her that in the eyes of society she does not deserve the happiness she is enjoying. Yet she is not willing for anyone else to have Angel and marries him without confessing her secret, although she has tried many times. When she does tell him her story, she is shocked to see that he is unable to forgive her. Although she accepts his decision to go away as her just desert and does her best while he is gone, she feels his treatment of her is cruel and hard. Her sins have never been intentional, and she feels her punishment, from Angel and others, has been persistent and unmerciful. But after her few days of joyous reunion with Angel, she is ready to die; she has had her share of happiness.

Tess's weakness lies in her feeling of responsibility for her family's welfare. She loves her younger brothers and sisters and feels she must provide for them. But this noble aim leads to most of her difficulties. Alec senses her concern for them and uses his generous gifts to them as a means of dominating Tess. She is grateful for what he does for the children, but does not want to be indebted to him. She fights against him, but the overwhelming burden of the large family is finally too much for her to bear alone.

Tess's love for Angel is all-encompassing and permanent. From their first meeting she is impressed with his manners and thenceforth looks upon him as a superior being. "To her sublime trustfulness he was all that goodness could be — knew all that a guide, philosopher, and friend should know. She thought every line in the contour of his person the perfection of masculine beauty, his soul the soul of a saint, his intellect that of a seer." His chivalrous, protective manner toward her contrasts so sharply with her former experience with men that she honors him to an excess. She strives to be like him in all ways.

Tess's loyalty to Angel during their separation is unwavering. She refuses to let anyone criticize him. She refuses to let either set of parents know her true circumstances for fear criticism will come to Angel. Her simplicity of faith in him is such that "even the most perfect man could hardly have deserved it."

The tragedy of Tess's life lies in the battle between "the inherent will to enjoy and the circumstantial will against enjoyment." After her brief affair with Alec, she is no longer a simple girl, but her experiences have failed to demoralize her soul. "Unexpended youth rises automatically within her after a temporary check bringing with it hope and an invincible instinct toward self-delight." Her loyalty to the man she loves, and the forbearance and nobility of her struggle against the fate which rules her life win the respect and sympathies of the reader.

ANGEL

Angel is an intruder into the Essex country life and is presented as a human being set apart from those around him. He is no longer comfortable with his clerical family because his semi-emancipated thinking has alienated him from their single-minded approach to life. He joins the agricultural community to prepare for his future life as a farmer, but he is treated as a temporary visitor who will soon be going on to a grander life.

Hardy uses the character of Angel to present many of the controversial subjects of the day. Angel cannot accept all the dogma of the church and therefore does not become a minister like his father. Those aspects of religion which deal with the supernatural are unacceptable to him. Although he shows great promise as a scholar, he does not go to the university because his father believes in education only as training for the ministry.

The distinction between religion and morality is a key element of Angel's part in the novel. He personifies the role convention can play in shaping one's destiny. Although intellectually liberated from orthodox Christianity, he is all the more dependent upon the Christian ethic and believes good morals are "the only safeguard for us poor human beings." Idealizing Tess into an essence of virgin purity, Angel is struck dumb when he learns that she, too, has sinned. Her confession strikes at the very foundation of his life. It is not until he removes himself from the society in which he has been raised, and sees morality in its temporal and transitory aspects, that he is able to accept Tess's character as one who wills good, no matter what the deeds.

It is ironic that Angel's first impression of Tess is that of a "fresh and virginal daughter of nature." As his love for her develops, it is apparent that he is loving an idealized woman rather than Tess. He feels it important to teach her history and literature and train her in speech and manners befitting a woman of society. He appreciates her abilities as a farm woman but is afraid to leave her for a few months for fear she might forget some of his training.

Angel's impulsive nature is seen many times in the story. That his heart outruns his head in declaring his love for Tess is made very clear. As he embraces her, he betrays his feelings with a "curious sigh of desperation."

He sees the inside of Tess's mouth one day as if it had been a snake's, signifying perhaps that Angel regards Tess as a temptress in the garden of the Talbothays. Seeking revenge on society, he asks Izz Huett to go to Brazil with him.

Angel considers himself to be a man of principle and of independent judgment, but his principles can be thrust aside when it suits his purpose. His reaction to old families illustrates this attribute. We are told he sees something sad in the extinction of a family of renown, but feels that wisdom and virtue should win respect rather than illustrious ancestors. Yet he rejoices when he learns that Tess is a d'Urberville; the simple, country girl comes from a more illustrious family than his own or those of his friends. After he learns that she is not a virgin, her family becomes a handle to despise her more. He reproaches himself for not forsaking her as soon as he found out about her ancestors in fidelity to his principles. After his experiences in Brazil when once again he can look upon Tess favorably, her historic family touches his sentiments and he sees it as an inconsequential accident.

It is difficult to sympathize with Angel for all his hardships during the year in Brazil. Self-centered and confused, he thinks only of his own dilemma. Upon his return to Wessex, he learns for the first time that Tess has not asked for money and that she may have suffered while he was away. He has not written to her nor inquired about her from his family.

Angel has no conception of Tess's love for him. He is amazed and horrified by her impulse to murder Alec. He thinks she has momentarily lost her mind. But tenderness is absolutely dominant in Angel at last and he becomes the protector she always believed him to be. Angel has not changed completely; he is still a slave to convention. When Tess suggests he marry 'Liza-Lu after she is gone, he is shocked by the idea of marrying his sister-in-law.

ALEC

Alec is the evil man in Tess's life, but he has good qualities and he comes through as more of a man than Angel does. His physical description would make him a typical villain in a melodrama. He is tall, with an almost swarthy complexion. A well-groomed, black moustache complete with curled points tops his badly molded, full lips. There are "touches of barbarism in his contours [and] a singular force...in his face and in his bold rolling eye."

Alec is sexually attracted to Tess from the very beginning. Accustomed to having his way with women, he is angered by her trifling with his feelings. He takes advantage of her innocence, exhaustion, and feeling of gratitude.

Alec realizes that concern for her brothers and sisters is Tess's weak spot and that by helping them he can put her in a position of indebtedness to him. Whatever his motives for helping her family, Alec does quite a bit for them in a material way and is more concerned for their welfare than Angel, who rather belatedly pays for John's headstone as his single contribution.

Alec admits that he is a bad sort of fellow, but can feel genuine remorse at the consequences of his actions. When he drives in such a reckless fashion that Tess refuses to ride with him, he is distressed at the sight of her walking such a distance. He is upset when Tess leaves him and drives like a madman to help her with her load if she won't come back to him. He is ready to pay for his deeds and urges Tess to write to him if she is in the least difficulty. When they meet again and Tess tells him of the child, he is struck mute.

Not enough of Alec's character is divulged to the reader to make his reappearance as a preacher believable. We have the feeling, rather, that he is merely another instrument in the hands of Fate working to thwart Tess. Supposedly the influence of Mr. Clare and the death of his mother result in his conversion, "perhaps the mere freak of a careless man in search of a new sensation." He travels about the countryside ranting a vehement form of Mr. Clare's views; his talents as an orator attract a good following. Now that he is converted, he wants to save everyone else: he employs the sign painter to cover every blank space with messages designed to reach the heart of sinners; he follows Tess in order to save her from the wrath to come. When Tess recites the thoughts of logical Angel, Alec's enthusiasm is stilled and he finds his position is untenable. He struggles to hold his shallow faith, but finds that his passion for Tess overwhelms all thoughts of carrying on his preaching. Once his faith is lost, he refuses the hypocrisy of preaching altogether. With a simple change of clothes and a shave, he is reconverted.

His attitude toward Tess is a combination of a desire to master her again and a genuine regard for her welfare. He is troubled by the sight of her agonizing labors on the Flintcomb-Ash farm, he rails against society for its cruel treatment of her family, and he offers to help her in a variety of ways. At the same time he is angry at her ingratitude and taunts her about her missing husband. He finally convinces her that her husband will never return and wins her back to him. But his fatal mistake is to carry on the taunts once Angel has returned and when he calls Tess's beloved by a foul name, she kills him.

TESS'S PARENTS

Many of Tess's problems can be traced to her parents, whose poverty and shiftlessness make it imperative that she leave her home to find employment at the d'Urbervilles.

Her father, John Durbeyfield, is described as a middle-aged man with rickety legs whose health is not very good. He was a life-holder on the cottage in which the family lived; his rank was above farm laborers, in a class with the artisans of the village. We are told that in days past he had cows and chickens, but his drinking and irregular energy for work led to the decline in family fortunes. He is a haggler when we first meet him, dependent upon an old horse for his livelihood. But shiftless as he is, he doesn't blame Tess for the death of the horse. He works harder digging a grave for him than he has worked for months growing a crop for the family.

John's life is changed by the revelation that he is a descendant of the noble d'Urbervilles. He begins to live as he deems proper for a titled man as soon as he hears of his pedigree. No longer does he consider it proper to slave at common labor. He spends his time thinking of ways to restore his family name to its former grandeur: Tess might marry a gentleman; or he might sell his title to d'Urberville; or perhaps the antiquarians in that part of England might contribute to a fund on his behalf.

He is concerned about his reputation. When Tess returns home, he worries about what his friends will say. His concern for the family name makes him refuse to admit the parson the night that Sorrow dies.

Joan is reasonably happy because she refuses to think very much about life in general. She has the happy intelligence of a child and an elastic spirit which bounces back after every setback whether it be the loss of a crop or the damaged reputation of her daughter. In contrast to Tess, who has received some education at the village school, Joan is steeped in superstition and folklore.

Joan is vain and witless. She prides herself on her pretty face and is proud that Tess has inherited her good looks. She has visions of a fine marriage for her daughter and encourages her daughter to go to work for the good-looking and wealthy d'Urberville. She thinks her daughter a fool for not marrying Alec but is gratified by even a dashing flirtation between them. She tells Tess not to tell Angel about her past and considers her daughter stupid when she does.

Joan has given birth to many children, and though she loves them dearly, she does not feel a great responsibility for them. Her labors are not onerous to her, for she postpones them from one day to the next. She does not begrudge Tess her happiness or pleasures and enjoys occasional hours at the inn away from her children. She loves to sing, learns songs easily, and teaches many to Tess.

She is almost as impressed as her husband at the nobility of the family, and when forced to move, she decides to go to Kingsbere, where the great family vaults lie.

ANGEL'S PARENTS

Hardy says nothing about the physical appearance of Angel's parents but draws their characters with a loving and favorable hand. Their singleness of purpose, their simple Christian lives, help us to understand Angel's background and the kind of thinking he can no longer accept.

His parents are described as a self-denying pair who forget their own needs and those of their family in trying to help needy parishioners. Although they would have liked Angel to marry the daughter of their friend, they keep an open mind regarding Tess and reserve liking for her until they can meet her. Had Tess followed through on her plan to visit them, she would have enlisted their sympathy, for their hearts went out toward extreme cases. When they learn of Tess's sin, their tenderness is instantly excited.

Angel's mother is more of a snob than his father. She is concerned whether Tess is of a good family and later urges Angel not to be anxious about a "mere child of the soil." She is disappointed when Angel comes home without his bride and instinctively asks if Tess's history will bear investigation. Accepting Angel's lie on this score, she tells him that since Tess is pure and chaste, she would have been refined enough for her. She feels sure that Angel's companionship and tuition will help Tess overcome any crudeness of manner.

Mr. Clare is a well-known parson in Wessex. His fame extends beyond his own parish, for he has affected the lives of many people. He is of the Low Church school, Evangelical, and is regarded as extremist even by his contemporaries. He wins the admiration of all for his thoroughness and his great energy in applying his principles. A man of apostolic simplicity in life and thought, he is known as good, kind, sincere, and the "earnestest" man in all Wessex. He is sanguine as a child, and he prays for Alec and other sinners.

He wins the respect of Angel by the way he lives his life and for his unworldliness. He never once inquires whether Tess is wealthy or penniless; his major concern is whether she has a Pauline view of humanity.

In his youth, Rev. Clare made up his mind once and for all on the "deeper questions of existence and admitted no further reasoning on them. He exercised great thrift so that his three sons could go to the university as preparation for entering the ministry. He does not feel it right to give his unbelieving son academic advantages which might be used to work against doctrines to which Rev. Clare has devoted his life. He is uncompromising—his fixed ideas cannot be altered—but he secretly mourns over his treatment of Angel and his "self-generated regrets are far bitterer than the reproaches" his wife occasionally expresses. He has a strong sense of justice, however, and sets aside a sum every year for Angel to purchase or lease land.

Despite his narrowness, Mr. Clare is described as far less "starched and ironed" than his older sons (who are caricatures of the conventional university graduate). Mr. Clare has the gift of charity to the full and lives an exemplary life.

GLOSSARY

Chapter 1

haggler	a huckster, peddler
black-pot	a sausage made of fat and blood

Chapter 2

Cerealia	observances in honor of Ceres
clipsing	embracing, hugging
colling	embracing, hugging

Chapter 3

fess	conceited
mommet	a dressed-up figure; a doll, puppet

larry	excitement
plim	swell
volk	folk
concretions	solid mass formed by aggregation and cohesion of particles

Chapter 4

sumple	supple
stubbard-tree	an early codling apple

Chapter 5

crumby	(slang) plump, and in good condition; buxom

Chapter 6

colorifuge	that which banishes or mitigates grief

Chapter 12

teave	strive, toil, labor

Chapter 13

Robert South	(1634-1716) English clergyman and author

Chapter 14

stopt-diapason (stopped diapason)	one (of two) principal foundation stops in an organ
deal	made of plain, unfinished wood

Chapter 15

Jeremy Taylor	(1613-1667) English prelate and author

Chapter 16

barton	farmyard

Chapter 17

Cowcumber	Cucumber
Tay	tea
nott	not
tranter	one that does odd jobs of hauling and peddling, usually with a horse and cart

Chapter 18

Hodge	an English rustic or farm laborer

Chapter 19
blooth   bloom, the stage of blossoming
niaiseries   simplicities, foolishnesses

Chapter 21
pummy   ground apples in process of cider making

Chapter 24
tract   a space or expanse of land, stretch or extent
                                of territory

Chapter 25
devolution   transference from one person to another

Chapter 31
baily   bailiff; district under the jurisdiction of bailiff
                                or baily

Chapter 33
randy   a noisy merrymaking or revel
partie carree   a party of four

Chapter 34
harridans   a worn-out strumpet; a vixenish woman, a
                                hag
withy   willow; a flexible branch of willow used for
                                tying or binding

Chapter 43
lanchets ⎱
lynchets ⎰   a strip of land left unplowed and untilled

flossy   styles of the pistillate flowers of maize silk
thirtover   that thwarts or obstructs; obstructive

Chapter 47
rick   a stack of hay, corn, peas, etc., especially one
                                regularly built and thatched; a mow

Chapter 48
nammet-time   luncheon, slight meal

Chapter 50
hart   stag

Chapter 58
trilithon   a prehistoric structure consisting of three large stones, two upright and one resting upon them as a lintel.

SUGGESTED EXAMINATION QUESTIONS

1. What part does each of the following play in Tess's tragedy: (a) her parents, (b) Alec, (c) Angel?

2. Explain the relationship between Alec and the Durbeyfields.

3. What effect does the knowledge of the d'Urberville heritage have on: (a) Tess's parents, (b) Tess, (c) Angel?

4. How does Tess's life exemplify "the inherent will to enjoy and the circumstantial forces against enjoyment?"

5. Choose a scene in the novel which you consider especially noteworthy, and show how the author has presented it effectively.

6. To what extent does Hardy use characters to present an idea? Give examples.

7. Describe the effect of the setting on the action of the novel. Give examples.

8. Discuss the manifestations of Fate as they affect the life of Tess.

9. What is the significance of the minor characters and are they effectively drawn: (a) Tess's parents, (b) Angel's parents, (c) the dairymaids?

10. From your experience, which of these characters do you find more true to life: (a) Angel, (b) Alec, (c) Angel's father?

11. How would the story be different if: (a) Angel had danced with Tess when he first saw her, (b) Tess's letter had been received by Angel, (c) Tess had visited the Clares?

12. In what ways does Tess contribute to her own tragedy? Discuss.

13. Discuss Angel's relationship with his family.

14. What is the significance of Angel's sojourn in Brazil?

15. Compare and contrast the characters of Alec and Angel.

SELECTED BIBLIOGRAPHY

Abercrombe, Lascelles. *Thomas Hardy: A Critical Study*. New York: Mitchell Kennerly, 1922.

Beach, Joseph Warren. *The Technique of Thomas Hardy*. Chicago: University of Chicago Press, 1922.

Brown, Douglas. *Thomas Hardy*. New York: Longman's Green, 1954.

Cecil, Lord David. *Hardy the Novelist*. London: Constable and Co., 1943.

Chew, Samuel C. *Thomas Hardy, Poet and Novelist*. New York: Knopf, 1928.

Duffin, Henry C. *A Study of the Wessex Novels*. Manchester University Press, 1937.

Firor, Ruth A. *Folkways in Thomas Hardy*. Philadelphia: University of Pennsylvania Press, 1931.

Guerard, Albert J. *The Novels and Stories of Thomas Hardy*. Cambridge, Mass.: Harvard University Press, 1949.

Johnson, Lionel. *The Art of Thomas Hardy*. London: John Lane, The Bodley Head, Ltd., 1923.

McCullough, Bruce. *Representative English Novels*. New York: Harper and Brothers, 1946.

Wagenknecht, Edward. *Cavalcade of the English Novel*. New York: Henry Holt and Co., 1943.

NOTES